NEW TECHNOLOGY DEVELOPMENT STRATEGY

JOHN LOK

Made with ❤ on the Notion Press Platform
www.notionpress.com

Contents

Preface — *v*

Prologue — *vii*

1. Explaining Cost Saving And Supply And Demand Business Relationship — 1

2. Learning Invisible Hand Economic Method — 9

3. Manufacturing Robots Reduce Warehouse Cost — 11

4. Technology How Helps Businesses To Improve Employee Behavior — 15

5. Reengineering Management Science — 58

6. How Technology Influences Consumer Behavior To Bring Reduce Cost — 64

7. Outsource Saving Cost Strategy — 79

8. Internet Multi-level Marketing Saving Cost Strategy — 97

9. Fm How Helps Organizations To Avoid Resource waste — 116

10. Internet Technology Resource Strategy — 125

11. Us Space Science Research Organization (nasa) Knowledge Management Innovation Benefits — 131

Preface

Introduction

Nowadays, business society is experiencing high technology stage. Can human apply AI technology to help businessmen to reduce cost. Any businessmen must hope to learn how to reduce business cost in long time. The question is what methods can be real useful to help them to reduce long time cost aim. In nowadays business socical behavioral economic view, I shall indicate real useful business cost reducing methods in order to let businessmen can learn how to reduce their business costs in long term.

How and why technology may help human to improve talent job behavior ? What methods may help human to create clever as well as creative ability? What method may improve organizational performance ? I shall indicate robot technology invention how to train human creative ability , also I shall explain whether robot tool may help human to improve economy development or help businessmen to reduce cost, I shall explain what skills may help human to raise clever, I shall explain what method may help organizations to improve performance. Readers can learn new knowledge how to improve human development.

In my this book, I shall attempt to explain how and why human may apply AI machine or other methods to help our business activities to reduce long term cost. Readers can learn fresh behavioral economic knowledge whether businessmen may choose what methods to help them to reduce business cost.

Prologue

Content of table

Chapter 1 Explaining cost saving and supply and demand business relationship

The difference between past and nowadays economists their demand and supply economic theory explanation? p.2-7

Why cost saving and supply and demand have close relationship? p.8-24

Chapter 2 Learning invisible hand economic method

How may " inivisible hand " factor influence the smart phone manufacturer products demand number increase? p.25-30

Chapter 3 Manufacturing robots reduce warehouse cost

How manufacturing robots help warehouse to reduce cost ? p.31-35

Chapter 4 Technology how helps businesses to improve employee behavior

Human Behavioral network job brings social economic benefits p.36-44

What does human network job mean

Why human network job behavior may influence economy

Robots take our jobs behavioral and economy influences

Robot job behavior brings economy influences

Intellectual human economic behaviors p.45-58

What does intellectual human economic behaviors mean ?

The relationship between social change and human behavior

How human productive behavior may influence economic development

● New Zealand farmer individual wine productive behavior
● America high technological productive behavior
● China share market investing behavior

Why has any individual country have many people invest share behavior which can influence the country's macro consumption desire?

Can technology influence human shopping behavioral change?

Why and how human behavior may influence the country's economic growth or recession?

Technology how impacts human behavior changing?

How and why employees behaviors may influence economy development?

Robots invention whether they can help organizations to raise efficiencies or inefficiencies?

Why social behavior may influence organizational strategy needs to be changed ?

Reasons why human behavior may influence economic recession or growth ?

How employee behavior influences organizational development?

Artificial intelligent Human clever and art creating ability methods

Why does technology raise online products sale demand and reduces shops products sale demand?

Does car technological development reach mature stage to help economic development?

Chapter 5 Reengineering Management Science Method

How reengineering management science method may help organizations
to improve performance ? p.59-64

Chapter 6 How Technology Influences Consumer Behavior To Bring Reduce Cost

Can technology influence human shopping behavioral change? p.65-70

Chapter 7 Outsource saving cost strategy

How outsourcing strategy helps organizations

to reduce cost ? p.71-80

Chapter 8 Internet Multi-Level Marketing saving cost strategy

●

What are the differences between multi level

marketing and direct personal sale? p.81-105

●

Whether multi level marketing can assist

economic growth.

●

Why the internet has positive influence on direct

sale industry in multi level market to assist

economic growth.

●

Whether multi level marketing can influence
economic growth in poverty countries.

Chapter 9 FM how helps organizations to avoid resource waste
green building avoids resource waste p.106-110
facility management helps organizations to avoid resource waste p.111-115
Chapter 10
Internet technology resource strategy
Reasons internet is important intangible resource to e-educational organization p.116-123
Organization time resource efficient spending methods
Is time limited resource to organizations p.136-140
Chapter 11
US Space science research organization (NASA) knowledge management innovation benefits

Why does intangible resource may influence NASA organization success p.141-150
Global environment protection resource management strategy
Why does NASA need to be a learning organization?
knowledge management strategy to NASA

CHAPTER ONE

Explaining cost saving and supply and demand business relationship

The difference between past and nowadays economists their demand and supply economic theory explanation? Why cost saving and supply and demand have close relationship?

The law of supply and demand defines the relationship between the price of a given good or product and the willingness of people to either buy or sell it. Generally, as the price of a good increases, people are willing to supply more and demand less. These economists had explained economic demand and supply theory as below:

Philosopher John Locke is credited with one of the earliest written descriptions of this economic principle in his 1691 publication, Some Considerations of the Consequences of the Lowering of Interest and the Raising of the Value of Money. Locke addressed the concept of supply and demand as part of a discussion about interest rates in 17th-century England. Many merchants wanted the government to lower the cap on interest rates charged by private lenders so that people could borrow more money and thus purchase more goods. Locke argued that the free-market economy should set rates because government regulation could have unintended consequences. If the lending industry were left alone, interest rates would regulate themselves, Locke wrote: "The price of any commodity rises or falls by the proportion of the number of buyers and sellers."

Sir James Steuart's Inquiry into the Principles of Political Economy, published in 1796, was the first known printed use of the term "supply and demand." When Steuart wrote his treatise on political economy, one of his main concerns was the impact of supply and demand on laborers.

Adam Smith dealt extensively with the topic in his 1776 epic economic work, The Wealth of Nations. Often referred to as the Father of Economics, Smith explained the concept of supply and demand as an "invisible hand" that naturally guides the economy. According to Smith, the invisible hand is the automatic pricing and distribution mechanisms in the economy. Smith described a society in which bakers and butchers provide products that individuals need and want, providing a supply that meets demand and developing an economy that benefits everyone. It is important to note that Smith's ideas haven't gone without critique over the years since his ideas were first published, though. Over time, his ideas have been added to in order to represent the changing times and include concepts such as marginal utility, comparative advantage, entrepreneurship, the time-preference theory of interest, and monetary theory.

One of Marshall's most important contributions to microeconomics was his introduction of the concept of price elasticity of demand, which examines how price changes affect demand. In theory, people buy less of a particular product if the price increases, but Marshall noted that in real life, this behavior was not always true. The prices of some goods can increase without reducing demand, which means their prices are inelastic. Inelastic goods tend to include items such as medication or food that consumers deem crucial to daily life. Marshall argued that supply and demand, costs of production, and price elasticity all work together.

Nowadays economists they explain demand and supply economic theory, they have some different to past economists whose explanation as below:

How Does Supply and Demand Work? The law of supply and demand is a theory that explains the interaction between the sellers of a resource and the buyers of that resource. Generally, as price increases, people are willing to supply more and demand less and vice versa when the price falls. What does the bottom line mean. Despite the origins of the law of supply and demand beginning hundreds of years ago, it's still a topic frequently referenced and utilized today in economic theory and discussions. The theory has developed over time to accommodate recent technological and economical advancements, but the basic ideas of the theory remain largely the same.

Does demand depend on supply?

Supply and Demand Determine the Price of Goods and Quantities Produced and Consumed. Consumers may exhaust the available supply of a good by purchasing a given good or service at a high volume. This leads to an increase in demand. As demand increases, the available supply also decreases.

What does market demand depend on?

Market factors affecting demand of consumer goods. The demand for a good increases or decreases depending on several factors. This includes the product's price, perceived quality, advertising spend, consumer income, consumer confidence, and changes in taste and fashion.

Who controls the demand in supply and demand?

Supply and demand are in turn determined by technology and the conditions under which people operate. At one extreme, the market could be populated by a large number of virtually identical sellers and buyers (for example, the market for ballpoint pens).

What are the two laws of demand and supply?

The law of demand holds that the demand level for a product or a resource will decline as its price rises, and rise as the price drops. Conversely, the law of supply says higher prices boost supply of an economic good while lower ones tend to diminish it.

What factors affect demand and supply?

Price fluctuations are a strong factor affecting supply and demand. When a product gets expensive enough that the average consumer no longer feels it is worth it to buy the product, then the demand declines. This leads to cuts in production that will hopefully stabilize the product's value.

What factors affect demand and demand?

Demand may be defined as the quantity of a commodity that a consumer is able and willing to buy, at each possible price, over a given period of time. • Essential elements of demand are quantity, ability, willingness, prices, and period of time.

Which factors affect supply?

Generally, the supply of a product depends on its price and other variables such as the cost of production.

   a. Price. Price can be understood as what the consumer is willing to pay to receive a good or service. ...

b. Cost of production. ...

c. Technology. ...

d. Governments' policies. ...

e. Transportation condition.

How does supply and demand work together?

It's a fundamental economic principle that when supply exceeds demand for a good or service, prices fall. When demand exceeds supply, prices tend to rise. There is an inverse relationship between the supply and prices of goods and services when demand is unchanged.

What happens to supply when demand increases?

An increase in demand, all other things unchanged, will cause the equilibrium price to rise; quantity supplied will increase. A decrease in demand will cause the equilibrium price to fall; quantity supplied will decrease.

What is the theory of demand?

Demand theory describes the way that changes in the quantity of a good or service demanded by consumers affects its price in the market, The theory states that the higher the price of a product is, all else equal, the less of it will be demanded, inferring a downward sloping demand curve.

What are the 4 basic laws of supply and demand?

1) If the supply increases and demand stays the same, the price will go down. 2) If the supply decreases and demand stays the same, the price will go up. 3) If the supply stays the same and demand increases, the price will go up. 4) If the supply stays the same and demand decreases, the price will go down.

The different types of demand are as follows:

i. Individual and Market Demand: ...

ii. Organization and Industry Demand: ...

iii. Autonomous and Derived Demand: ...

iv. Demand for Perishable and Durable Goods: ...

v. Short-term and Long-term Demand:

What creates demand for a product?

You can create demand for a unique product if you can manage to solve a persistent problem for the consumer. People are always running away from pain, and providing them with an outlet is a sure-fire way to create massive demand for your goods.

What are the 7 factors that affect supply?

The seven factors which affect the changes of supply are as follows: (i) Natural Conditions (ii) Technical Progress (iii) Change in Factor Prices (iv) Transport Improvements (v) Calamities (vi) Monopolies (vii) Fiscal Policy.

What can affect demand?

Factors Affecting Demand

Price of the Product. ...

The Consumer's Income. ...

The Price of Related Goods. ...

The Tastes and Preferences of Consumers. ...

The Consumer's Expectations. ...

The Number of Consumers in the Market.

What are the three factors affecting demand?

The demand for a product will be influenced by several factors:

Price. Usually viewed as the most important factor that affects demand. ...

Income levels. ...

Consumer tastes and preferences. ...

Competition. ...

Fashions.

What are the 4 factors of supply?

The four factors that can shift the supply curve include natural conditions, input prices, technology, and government.

What causes increase in supply?

If the cost of production is lower, the profits available at a given price will increase, and producers will produce more. With more produced at every price, the supply curve will shift to the right, meaning an increase in supply.

What causes supply changes?

A change in supply is an economic term that describes when the suppliers of a given good or service alter production or output. A change in supply can occur as a result of new technologies, such as more efficient or less expensive production processes, or a change in the number of competitors in the market.

Is supply and demand a good strategy?

When it comes to profit placement, supply and demand zones can be a great tool as well. Always place your profit target ahead of a zone so that you don't risk giving back all your profits when the open interest in that zone is filled.

How is demand created?

Demand creation is a process that fuels the revenue pipeline so the sales team can meet or exceed their quotas. In other words, it takes your big idea — the creative appeal of your brand — and turns it into sales. That sounds a lot like demand generation, which often gets confused with lead generation.

What are the two parts of demand?

Economists define demand as the quantity of a good or service that buyers are willing and able to buy at all possible prices during a certain time period. Notice that there are two components to demand: willingness to purchase and ability to pay.

Can we control demand?

If you're willing to think and act strategically, you can easily manipulate the laws of supply and demand. It should be surprising to learn, however, that by manipulating the laws of supply and demand, you can make more profit in less time and with far fewer headaches

How do you control demand?

Here are five short-term actions to improve your demand variability management plans in this time of uncertainty:

Maintain transparent, proactive relationships with your suppliers. ...

Activate alternate sources of supply. ...

Reduce lead times. ...

Update inventory policy and planning. ...

Align supply and demand management.

What are the 8 types of demand?

There are 8 states of demand: negative demand, no demand, latent demand, falling demand, irregular demand, full demand, overfull demand and unwholesome demand.

What is Demand?

Types of Determinants of Demand. Every factor has a unique impact on demand. ...

Price of the Product. ...

The Income of the Consumers. ...

Number of Buyers in the Market. ...

Consumer's Expectations. ...

Tastes and Preferences of The Consumers. ...

Complement Goods. ...

Substitute Product.

What is theory of supply?

The law of supply is a fundamental principle of economic theory which states that, keeping other factors constant, an increase in price results in an increase in quantity supplied. In other words, there is a direct relationship between price and quantity: quantities respond in the same direction as price changes.

What are the types of supply?

There are five types of supply—market supply, short-term supply, long-term supply, joint supply, and composite supply.

Which comes first supply or demand?

Demand comes first and it's followed by the corresponding supplies. Supply and demand are both very important to economic activity. Supply is the total amount of a particular good or service available at a given time to consumers at a given price. Demand is a representation of a consumer's desire to purchase goods and services; it acts as a measurement of a consumer's willingness to purchase a specific good or service at a given price. These two economic forces influence each other; they are both important for the economy because they impact the prices of consumer goods and services within an economy and the quantities produced and consumed. Supply and demand are both keys to understanding the economy because they reflect the prices and quantities of consumer goods and services within an economy.

What are the relationship between demand and supply?

According to market economy theory, the relationship between supply and demand balances out at a point in the future; this point is called the equilibrium price.

Economists and companies analyze the relationship between supply and demand when making strategic product decisions. Both economists and companies analyze the relationship between supply and demand when making strategic product decisions. The assumption behind a market economy is that supply and demand are the best determinants for an economy's growth and health.

Consumer Behavior Influences Demand

One way that companies or economists might analyze this relationship is to create graphs that chart the equilibrium price of certain goods and services in order to determine product development and their production schedule. Consumer behavior dictates which products are produced and sold because consumers create the demand that companies attempt to meet. As a result, companies may study consumer behavior in an attempt to understand the current demand and predict future demand. It is vital that companies maintain the capacity to produce enough of a good or service that they can satisfy consumer demands.

Supply and demand are two sides of the same market coin. Generally, supply is how much of something is available or will be produced at a certain price. Demand is how much of something people want to purchase or consume at a certain price. One way to develop a more precise relationship between the two is to consider how the price of something affects its supply and its demand. Generally when the price of a good goes up, so does the supply, since firms are willing to create more when they can sell at higher prices. But when the price of a good goes up consumers will, at the same time, generally demand less. It is the interaction of supply and demand that determines how much will be produced and consumed and at what price, converging to a state known as equilibrium.

CHAPTER TWO

Learning invisible hand economic method

How may " inivisible hand " factor influence the smart phone manufacturer products demand number increase?

The invisible hand is for the law of supply and demand explains how the pull and push of these two factors serve to benefit sciety as a whole. In simple, every consumer choose to buy the product, he/she pursues to earn the most more interest to the manufacturer needs to produce the product as its product may be of the greatest value to let the consumer intends only his/her own gain, led by an invisible hand to promote the product to let the consumer to make satisfaction to choose to buy the product.

In behavioral economic view, the invisible hand to the product manufacturer may be " the consumer whose satisfactory feeling to use the product".So, the invisible hand meant that ir can not be touch , seen, it only brings feeling to let the consumer to feel. This feeling to the product is very mportant factor to excite the consumer to choose to buy the product, e.g. smart phone product the smart phone buyer's invisible hand factor may include: The smart phone can link to app to use internet service, download documents from smart phone , taking phonoes, watching movie, listening music, clock time etc. function, seeling different countries street locations, instead of general mobile talking function.

So, all of above factors will be future new smart phone main " invisible hand" factors to excite future smart phone buyers to make purchase decision to choose to buy the kind of smart phone among different kinds of smart phone products innovation , when they are manufactured to promote to smart phone market to sell.

So, in smart phone market supply and demand view, the smart phone manufacturer needs to innovate new smart phone products in order to let smart phone buyers fee its news phone buyers feel itsnew smart phone products have unique functions or features to excite its smart phone buyers to choose to buy its new kind of smart phone products, because smart phone buyers will be influences to make final smart phone purchase decision by invisible hand factors from smart phone different new function .

Smart phone manufacturers need to innovate many new functions o future new kinds of smart phone manufacturing in order to bring new invisible hand satisfactory feeling to let any one smart phone buyer to feel whose new smart phone can bring the most unique satisfactory feeling to let them to feel. So, smart phone 's invisible hand factor is main influential factor to bring smart phone manufacturer's new smart phone demand number will increase or decrease. If the smart phone manufacturer can often innovate its smart phone products to let smart phone buyers feel more using satisfactory feeling to its new kind of smart phone more than its other similar kinds of smart phone manufacturers. Then, the smart phone manufacturer ought raise its smart phone purchase number demand easily.

What is smart phone opportunity cost?

Hence, the concept of opportunity cost factor means smart phone manufacturers need to forgone opportunities of time cost , design new kinds of smart phone products, e.g. smart phone pictures, colour and shape , future smart phone manufacturers need to concentrate more time to research how to innovate new featurers and function to let every potential smart phone buyers to bring more functions using satisfactory feeling in order to attract they choose to buy its smart phone product.

On conclusion, opportunity cost to smart phone manufacturers may be forgone spend more time on smart phone design, colour choice, shape choice aspects. Smart phone manufacturers need to spend more time on innovate new feature and function aspects in order to satisfy future smart phone using needs in global competitive smart phone smart.

CHAPTER THREE

Manufacturing robots reduce warehouse cost

How manufacturing robots help warehouse to reduce cost ?

What does AI prediction machine mean? Why AI machine can make more accurate economic prediction to compare human economists? How to apply AI machine to make more accurate economic prediciton to compare human economists? In tradition, economists can gather data to make statistics to analysis how to predict this year or next year either economic growth or recession occurrence in possible. But, since AI machine tool, it can apply to manufacturing, service , logistic , office, hospital, shopping center etc. difference business working environment aspects, whether it can help economists to make more economic prediction in possible or economists will need AI machine to help them to make more accurate economic prediction for businessmen or societies needs. I shall attempt to give evidence to explain as
below:

Economists view our world is differently than most people. Businessmen are influenced everything by forces such as supply and demand, production and consumption, prices and costs economic concept.
However, AI machine is needed to everywhere, such as packed into your smart phones apps, warehouse logistic workers, non manual vehicles. So, AI machine may innovate our lives. Human needs AI machine to assist our tasks from complex to simple. Businessmen may bring economic time and saving long time cost benefits. Such as online shopping method, AI can help consumers find any kinds of different products prices and photos to compare in order to make reasonable purchase decision more easily from webstores channel as well as businessmen can apply ecommerce sale channel to help them to sell products to different countries in short time.

Prediction is being used for traditional tasks in business environment, such as inventional management and demand and supply forecasting. For example, because the smart phone seller predicts smart phone buyers number will reduce when he feels every family, old and young age adult who have owned at least one smart phone to every family in the country. SO, the smart phone seller ought reduce to manufacture and sell the old smart phones in order to avoid the kind of old smart phone price to reduce, due to the kind of smart phone demand purchase number will reduce,but he ouhgt to continue to innovate new kind of smart phone in order to supply new innovative smart phones products to satisfy future smart phone users needs. It is general economists judgement.Such as this smart phone case, when smart phone prediction is cheap, there has two simple economic forces drive the new opportunities, such as new kind of innovative smart phones need that predction new kind of innovative smart phones will be needed to creat in order to keep this smart phone manufacturer competitive ability in the country.

However, at low levels, a prediction machine, such as AI machine can relieve humans of predictive tasks and save on costs, when AI machine help economists or businessmen to do gather this smart phone manufacturer to manufacturing and selling this kind of smart phones data in this country consumption market every day. AI machine can gather data in short time and then it can give this kind of smart phone manufacturing and sale number data to this smart phone company every day in order to make statistic conclusion. So, AI will affect the economic of a business so dramatically, that they will no longer be used to simply enchance productivity in executing against the strategy, they will help this smart phone manufacturewr to change the strategy itself, such as whether
it ought continue to improve or innovate another kind of new smart phone design and function in order to satisfy future smart phone users needs. So, smart phones daily manufacturing and selling data is the most influential point to help this smart phone manufacturer to make decision whether it is the right time to innovate its another new kind of smart phone design and function or not in order to keep its smart phone sale competitive ability in this country.

Amazon can apply AI machine to help it reduces warehouse seeking goods time from shelves. Because Amazon has many shevles, it putted many kinds of products in shelves. Every one of worker will need long time to seek the kind of goods in order to transport to customers when they had bought the kind of goods. Amazon found this long time seeking goods problem to avoid transport time waste. It applied AI transport machine to help human worker to seek any kinds of goods from shelves. On consequently, AI transport machine help every warehouse worker to reduce at least 5 to 10 minutes to seek ths right kind of product from shelves. So, if the warehouse has 600 different kinds of products to prepare to transport to global buyers homes in the day. Every product seeking time from shelves will reduce 600 x 5 minutes or 600 x 10 minutes seeking time. So, this 600 different kinds of products will reduce 3,000 minutes or 6,000 minutes transport time to deliver to global buyers homes. So, AI machine had helped Amazon to reduce goods transport time in this day. It can help Amazon bring economic transport time shorten benefits to let global buyers can get their products within the day or tomorrow rapidly. In this case, AI machine help Amazon 's business model from shopping -then -shipping to shipping -then -shopping , AI helps Amazon to avoid buyers whose purchase goods return occurrence chance when they can be transported to their homes in short time. and accelerates the timing of investment.

Hence, it seems that AI machine may help businesses to bring these economic benefits: mahcine learning is often referred to as advances in artificial intelligence because systems prediction on this technique learn and improve over time, these systems produce significantly more accurate predictions than human economists or businessmen, traditoinal statistics methods require the articulation of hypotheses or at least of human economists analysis. In fact, AI technology is called " machine learning) for a reason. The mahines leearn form data. The prediction machine has to learn how the data is associated with actual incidences of irregular heart problem, such as Amazon transport time reducing case, when Amazon discover it will have many buyers choose either goods return decision more than non -goods return decision. AI mahcine help Amazon to seek goods from shelves to avoid goods long time seeking from human workers when AI transport delivery machine help human workers to do " goods seeking from shelves tasks working first step, then human worker only need to spend time to put the goods to lorry to transport to lorries to drive to airport in order to fly the goods to overseas customers in second time. So, AI machine may help Amazon to gather warehouse different kinds of goods shelves location data any where in order to help human workers to reduce goods seeking timr from shelves. AI mahcine may Amazon warehouse workers to avoid to spend long time to seek goods from shelves, they can concentrate on spending time to put goods on lorries.Also, AI machine help Amazon to reduce warehouse workers number or reduce salaries expenditure, when AI warehouse machine can replace human workers to do goods seeking tasks from shelves.

Ai machine help organizaitons to achieve new division of labour aim. Such as, a law firm may apply AI mahcine help human lawyers to take legal documents and predicted which

information was condfidential. This product is valuable to law firms because when they are required to disclose documents, they have to black out comnfidential information. Historically,

redaction was done by hand, with humans reading documents and blacking out confidential information. SO, AI machine help lawyers to save time and effort. Such as Amazon case, AI machine

creates new division of labor strategy in any one of Amazon warehouse. AI machine will concentrate time on doing " goods seeking tasks from shelves in first step", then human workers will concentrate on time on doing " goods are putting on lorries tasks in second step ". Traditoinal , warehouse workers need to spend time to do seek goods from shelves task and putting goods to lorries tasks both. Nowadays,warehouse AI machine only need to spend time to do seek goods from shelves task , but human workers only need to spend time to do goods are putting to lorries tasks. So, AI machine will change traditional divisoin of labor to warehouse tasks in the future. Because AI machine will help workers to reduce goods transportation time and reducing goods return chance occurrence.

CHAPTER FOUR

Technology how helps businesses to improve employee behavior

Explaining the relationship between increasing proficient workers number and avoiding excess resource waste

In organizational behavioral economic view, whether they have cause and effect relationship between employees how to use resources behaviors and organizational resource excess use within organizations ?

In organizational behavioral economic view, whether they have cause and effect relationship between employees how to use resources behaviors and organizational resource excess use within organizations. For example, if the organization has many employees number, whether the organization will use its any internal tangible and intangible resources easily per day.

For construction organization example, one construction organization must need to buy different kinds of construction materials to prepare to let workers to help it to manufacture different kinds of properties or houses (products) in order to sell to property buyers. In its every building construction site, it will need more or less workers, they are needed to use different kinds of construction materials to build housess in different construction sites. I assume that construction site (A), it has 100 construction workers number, every day, construction site (A) 100 workers need to use different kinds of construction materials to help them to build 3 building floors wall at least floor number in the construction site (A).

I assume that these 100 construction workers , they include proficient workers and not proficient workers. For proficient construction workers group, they have 50 number, and not proficient construction workers group, they also have 50 number . Hence, the proficient construction workers only need to spend 3 hours maximum and use less number of constructoin materials, then they can finish to build 3 building floors wall per day.

I also assume that all constructoin material supply number is limited. It means that due to this construction firm needs to pre-booking to purchase this kind of the best quality of constructoin material from overseas before three worths. So, it must not have enough time to pre-booking to purchase this kind of best quality of constructoin materials when they are used rapaidly within one month, due to this one month is the final finishing time to this construction firm within one month. Hence, limited construction material supply number and limited finishing time to build this new 40 floors house within this final one month .

So , not proficient construction workers number , limit number of construction material and per day 8 hours which is its limited resources in behavioral eocnomy view. Moreover, total 50 proficient and not proficient 50 construction workers (human resource employees number) will cause this constructoin firm , it will possible need to build this new 40 floors house are more than one month, if these 50 proficient construction workers , they have more than 30 at least number, they are absent to cause their overall construction workers' efficiency to be fallen down, due to the other 50 not proficient constuction numbers must need their teaching how to cooperate ad how use less materials to build this new 40 floor hourse rapidly in order to raise overall constructon team efficiency and avoid to delay more than one month time to build this 40 floors new house successfully within this final one month time.

Hence, it explains that when one organization has more employees, it does not represent that this organization must need to use more resource to achieve its any mission, such as this construction firm case, although it has 50 not proficient construction workers, they need to use more construction materials to build this new 40 floors house in this construction site (A). But, in fact, it has other 50 proficient construction workers, they know how to reduce construction materials to build every building floor wall for this new 40 floors building house. So, they can teach the not proficient building workers to know hoe to avoid to use extra excess constructon material to finish to construct every building fllor wall. SO, although, it has 50 not proficient construction workers number, but they can be taught to learn how to reduce to use these limited the best quality of construction materials to build this 40 floors new house. It implies that if the construction workers number can increase, e.g. increases more 50 not proficient construction workers, this the best quality of construction material resource number must not need to increase demand, because this construction site (A) has 50 proficient construction workers , they can teach these 50 not proficient construction workers how to avoid to use extra excess this kind of high quality construction material to build this new 40 floor house efficiently and effectively within this one month.

Hence, if this construction firm won't have more than 30 proficient workers number is absent in this final one month, it will have enough proficient construction workers to teach these 50 not proficient construction workers to know how to use this high quality of construction materials to build this 40 floors new house building in order to avoid waste or construction material need shortage challenge occurs in this final one month time.

Consequently , it ought finish to build this 40 floors new house building within this month. Hence, it explains why its this kind of high quality of construction material resource need must not increase, because if its all proficient construction workers is absent and their absent number is less than 30, then they have enough proficient construction workers number , they can teach this 50 not proficient construction workers how to avoid to use extra excess construction materials resource number in order to have enough construction material resource supply to satisfy this new 40 floors building house to finish construction within one month finishing date need. On conclusion, in organizational behavioral economic view, it explains that resource use need must not be influenced to increase when the organization's employees number increase. It depends on whether the organization has how many talent and proficient workers number in order to assist them and teach the not proficient employees how to use resource to manufacture any kinds of products in order to avoid to spend extra excess of resource need. Hence, organizational behavioral economic view, it can explain that any organization's increase to employees number, it does not mean that its resource number is also needed to increase. Moreover, in organizational behavioral economic view, it also explains that if the organization can have many proficient workers to help it to do any complex tasks, they will help it to bring avoiding waste or excess extra resource to use advantage, because they ought know whether how they work, they can help the organization to improve performance or raise efficiency e.g. car manufacture, computer manufacture, television manufcture etc. home electronic products or car leisure products. Due to that manufacturre processes are complex, if the organization can have more proficient high skillful workers to help it to manufacture their products. They ought help it to use lesser manufacturing time and less manufacturing resource to finish any above these products to compare not proficient or low skillful manufacture workers. So, in long time, the organization must may earn economic low cost benefits from proficient worker individual high manufacturing skillful knowledge behavior or performance. So, organizational behavioral economic theory explains why even the organization plans to increase employees number, it's resources number won't be influenced to increase rapidly because when the organization's proficient high skillful workers number is more 2 times at least than not proficient low skillful workers number. They ought have enough effort to train and teach and cooperate with the not proficient low skillful manufacture workers to improve their manufacture skills in order to raise manufacturing efficiency and reduce extra excess resources waste and avoid to bring long term resource waste economic loss. So, any manufacturing organizations must need to increase proficient workers number to assist the not proficient low skillful workers to learn how to improve their skills and know how to reduce to use excess resources to keep to manufacture the highest number of products aim frequently. Consequently, the organization will bring long term low resource use manufacturing economic benefit.

Human Behavioral network job brings social economic benefits

What does human network job mean ? Why may human network job be popular? Why human network job behavior may influence economy ?
Nowadays internet is popular to use. We can apply internet to find data , search any new things, even earn money. Why does internet
may become huma network job source. For example, e-publish may be one kind of new human network job. Any authors may apply internet
channel to help them to sell electronic or paper books from e-publisher web store. They may apply facebook, you tub etc. any online
channel to promote themselves new books to let new readers to know whether when they may buy themselves favourable new topic books to read

from electronic publisher web store.

Thus, future electronic publisher industry may help any authors to build internet network platform to help them to sell and promote ot advertise their any one new electronic or paper book topic to let global any one reader to choose to buy their any new topic books from electronic publisher web store easily and conveniently. However, it implies that electronic network platform author may be one kind of future new human network job in our societies.

How electronic network platform author job may bring economy benefit in macro economy view? A person can have few friends, contacts and still be very influential if these few

friends and contacts are themselves highly influential, e.g. one author must not need to know any one reader in global society. When they like to choose any electronic books from electronic internet network platform. They may become the author's any one topic book buyer, when they feel the author's any one topic book is fun and attract they make decision to buth the strange author whose the topic book from electronic book publisher's platform web store conventiently in short time. Although, they are strangers, they do not know themselves , but the reader can understand what it way that made Google from writing platofrm to create new creative mind and typing network job method to replace traditional hand writing book method for global authors. It will be one kind of new human network writing job.

Hence, global any one reader can apply an innovative search engine , such as google.com to find whether whom author personal new topic books are value to read from internet.

Then, the electroniuc publisher's web store may be new book store platform sale network to help the author to sell many electronic or paper books from electronic network platform

in short time. So, internet may be future new network plaform to help global any one author to create network writing job absolutely. Furthermore, internet may be popular social media

to help any one author to build goold relationship between his/her readers. It is one kind of new network, human network job. New authors do not need to buy many paper books to prepare to put in any one book shop warehouse. Their every book can print on demand to reduce out of book stock in any one book shop. They may choose to sell either electronic books or paper books both from any one book publisher web store. So, electronic network platform may be one kind of good writing channel to help human authors to create income and it can also help authors to bring new creative mind and new topic fun content books to let readers to know and buy to read from electronic publisher network platform.

Why does human behavior may be one kind of new human network job to bring global economic advantages. ALthough, it may be free income or without inocme, but the person does the network behavior, his/her behavior may be bring advantages to influence many other people's health. For this case, when a worker in a coffee shop in an airport gets a vaccination aganinst the flu, it does not only helps him or her stay healthy, but also helps the many travellers who might otherwise have been inflected if that workers caught the flu. So, the externality , the result implies the vaccination of even a part of a community conveys benefits to the whole community. For example, governments pay special attention to the vaccinations of school children, teachers, health mothers, and the elderly, categories of people particularly susceptible not only to catching, but also to transmitting a disease.

It is not accidential that governments are heavily involved with vaccination . When there are externalities, free market, fail to persuade individual incentives with society's
their the worker's decision of whether to get a vaccine ends up attracting whether other people get sick. The workers might not fully take all these other people's potential suffering into account when making her or his vaccination decision.

As Stanford University does many suggestions, understand this and tries to help them make the right decisions and so providers free flu vaccines for its staff and students.
Small pockets of unvaccinated individuals can allow a disease to gain a spread more widely well-being. For example, parent weighing the costs and benefits of a vaccine for their child is not always thinking of the consequences of that vaccination to other people. THese are markets in which subsidizing or regulating behavior can make everyone better off. Because the reason for requiring that a child be vaccinated before enrolling in school is not just to protect that child, because each child's vaccination affects others via potential contagions.

Robots take our jobs behavioral and economy influences
Robot job behavior brings economy influences

If one day robots can replace human to do simple, even complex jobs. They will bring what influences to our global societial economy.The popular economic refrain declares that the
global middle class is dying and robots will soon take our jobs, e.g. shopping

center customer service jobs, library service jobs, cinema ticket sale jobs, restaurant kitchen cooker jobs,
even, bus drivers, taxi drivers etc. public transport driving jobs, accountant, doctors etc. professional jobs. Whether it is beautiful or petty matter if our future societies have many human jobs can be replaced to do from robots. Businessman must may reduce to employ employees and reduce to pay salary or wage, when robots can be replaced to do their employees tasks. But, societies must bring unemployement rate rises , due to societies will have many people loss jobs when their employers choose to buy robots to serve their clients or do any office tasks or customer service or cleaning etc. tasks.

In micro economy view, employers may save money in long term, but in macro economy view, it will cause unemployment ratio rises , even crime rate rises when there are many people lose
jobs in societies. These models of doom, though, fail to account for the hundreds of businesses riding the waves of change in their industries when robots may be invented to replace human to do many simple , even complex tasks in our future societies.

WE may image that one small factory needs to manufacture fishes canes to sell to supermarket, the small , cheaper stuff and higher margin parts of the fishes manufacture industry. Before, this factory needs to employe many human factory workers need to help every fresh customer makeing the perfect fishing gear, designed for performance, durability, and cost in order to achieve to manufacture every fish cane in whole fished processing manufacturing stages. Every worker needs to spend about 15 to twenty minutes to finish every fish cane , till to delivery to any supermarket to sell. If this fish canes manufacturing factory can apply manufacturing robots to help them to finish any one working tasks , every robot can only spend five minutes to finish whole fresh fish cane manufacturing process. Thus, every robot can
help this factory save 10 to 15 minutes time to finsh every fish cane manufacturing process. IN fact, time is money, because when every robot can help this factory to reduce 10 to 15 minutes time to compare human worker. Then, this factory can finish about 20 fish canes in one hour if it can use robot to help it to manufacture fish canes. Otherwise, if this factory still use human workers to help it to manufacture fish canes, then it can finsh about 3 to 4 fish canes in one hour. SO, the manufacturing efficiency ensures that robots must help this fish manufacturing factory to

raise fish canes number more than human workers. So, in robotic behavioral economy view, manufacturing robots must help this fish canes manufacturing factory to raise fish canes manufacturing number and deliver increasing number to supermarkets to prepare to sell every day. Robots can help this fish canes manufacturing factory bring manufacturing time saving, rising manufacturing efficiency, improving performance and reducing wages expenditure long time advantages in micro economy view. However, manufacturing robots can also bring disadvanages to society, e.g. increasing unemployment ratio, increasing crime rate,

this factory workers will lose jobs and income, they need earn social welfare from government and increasing government finance pressure in short time, even long time in macro economic view.

Stanford University graduate program in economics, Scott lecturer explained that "in demand and supply economic theory for robots supply and demand case, robots supply number increasing may influence human workers demand number decrease. It sometimes calls " the efficient frontier".

No specific human beings were mentioned in any of economics classes. As robots supply and demand in market case, They (robots) may be purely theoretical " agents" who reached to the most reasonable sale prices in order to persuade any one businessman buyer to make manufacturing robot buying decision whether robots can help him / her to bring how much saving time , saving money, saving cost, improving performance, efficiency economic benefit before he/she plans to reduce workers number when he/ she decides to apply robots to replace human workers in his/her factory or office or any service department, e.g. cinema ticket sale service, shopping center customer service, shopping center cleaning , supermarket customer service etc. service or sale tasks. When robots can replace human to do any one of these tasks in any organizations. So, robots may be human worker agents who reached to prices the way robots would react to a software command. There was nothing that explained why some people thrived and others did n't or why truly brilliant, hardworking people could fail when much lazier folks succeeded." Having been admitted to the Stanford University graduate program in economics, Scott lecturer hoped to get his answers there.

How robots influence our future social changing? Using the right technology can be a boon to your business in this economy. For internet example, it is easier than ever to find well-matched customers all around the world, to stay in contact with them, and to more quickly design the products they want. If you focus solely on being cutting -edge, though you risk letting the technology

take over what should be very robust relationships with your customers , employees, and colleagues. IN nowaddays society, technoligical advances and cutomation, personal

relationships in business are more crucial than ever. I mean that robots can not replace human to serve clients to let them to feel more comfortable and passion more easily. For shoe shop case example, if the shoe shop apply one robot to serve its clients to replace human shoe salesperson to serve its shoe customers. Robots ensure that they can not persuade every shoe potential buyer to make shoe buying decision more easily when robots need to contact every shoe potential buyer. The reason is simple, because robots can not touch any one shoe buyer individual emotion very easier.

If the shoe buyer needs the robots to help him/her to choose any right shoe styles when he/she can not feel himself / herself can make the most right shoe style choice decision. The robots can not replace human shoe salesperson to make shoe style choice judgement more easily. They must need longer time to analyze whether which shoe style may be the most suitable to the shoe buyer. Otherwise, human shoe salesperson may attempt to make the most right shoe style choice decision to help any one shoe buyer to chooce the most right style shoe because he/she owns shoe style sale experience, shoe style knowledge, the most important reason is that they can feel every shoe customer individual emotion to touch whether he/she will feel comfortable or happy when they attempt to help every shoe customer to seek the most right shoe style in every shoe customer whole shoe searching processing. Othwerwise, serving robots are only one machine, they can not touch or feel every shoe customer individual emotion whether he/she feel comfortable or unhappy or happy when they need to contact them in whole shoe searching processing. Hence, I believe that some tasks robots can

not repalce human staff to do very easily. Otherwise, robots may bring disadvanatges to let any one businessman to loss his/her customers, due to robots can not touch every customer

emotion to compare human staff in service tasks more easily. Robots serving customer behaviors may cause money lose and customers number lose to the shop in micro economic view.

Intellectual human economic behaviors

What does intellectual human economic behaviors mean ? I believe that when we choose or decide to do intellectual behaviors, then our societies will be influenced to bring economic growth in consequence.I shall attempt to indicate pollution case to explain how and why eithet our intellectual or foolish behaviors may bring economic growth or recession in consequence as below:

On one hand, for air pollution social case aspect example, if we only consider to buy cars to drive for working aimr or holiday leisure aim. Then, our societies air will be polluted. Our health will be influenced to bad. Our car driving behaviors may cause global environment air pollution serously. In long tiem, global air pollution will bring our bodies health to be bad. Although, ourselves car driving behaviors may bring our driving travelling leisure enjoyment and comfortable feeling in short time, also we so not need to pay public transport fare often, but we need to compensate ourselves health economic intangible loss due to air pollution , when cars number increases, dirty air will cause ouselves health to become bad.

In the result, we will need to pay more medical expenditure when we are old age, due to ourselves bodies will become bad, due to we breathe global dirty air every day, due to ourselves cars pollute air in long time, e.g. 10 to 20 years, even 30 more without limited air pollution environment. So, driving cars behavior may be one kind of human foolish behavior and our foolish behavior may bring ourselves future long time medical expenditure absolutely.

One the other hand, water pollution social aspect, if we often keep much rubblish to pollute sea, oil exploration porcessing pollute ocean , ships gas pollute ocaen, then fishes will eat polluted food and drive dirty water, due to global ocean is polluted.

In fact, because human only to conside how to buy boats to carry on leisure enjoyment activities, or catch cruises to travel on the sea. Also, oil manufacturers only consider researching anywhere to find new oil exploration places to manufacture oil product, when their oil exploration processes pollute ocarn . Consequently, global fishes drink polluted warer or eat polluted food. They will have poison. SO, human will have high chance to eat poison polluted fishes, due to fishes are poison or are polluted.

So, human is doing foolish activities, we only hope to find oil exploration places to pollute ocean or we only spend money to buy ticket to catch ships to travel anywhere in global ocean. All of these human foolish behaviors will bring pollution to global ocean. On consequently, we will need to compensate to eat polluted or dirty or poision fishes, ourselves bodies health will be bad. In long time, we need have high chance to pay medical expenditure when we are old. So, pollution case may be one good example to explain how and why human foolish behavior may influence ourselves future need to compensate serious medical loss.

All of these human foolish behavior will bring pollution to global ocean. On consequently, we will need to compensate to eat polluted or dirty or poison fished , ourselves bodies health will be bad. In long time, we will have high chance to pay medical expenditure, when we are old. So, pollution case may be one good example to explain how and why human ourselves intellectual or foolish behaviors may influence future long time economic loss or economic growth or recession in micro and micro economic view.

On another water pollution aspect hand, if we often keep rubbish to sea, oil exploration processing pollutes ocean and ships' gas pollute ocean, then fishes will eat polluted food and drink dirty water, due to fishes will eat polluted food and drink dirty sea water because the global ocean is polluted seriously.

In fact, because human only consider how to buy boats to carry on any leisure water activities, or catches cruises to travel on the sea. Also, oil manufacturers only consider any where to find oil exploratin places to manufacture oil products from ocean, when their pol exploration processes can plooute ocean. Consequently, global fishes drink polluted water or eat direty food. They will have poison. So, human will have high chance to eat poison fishes.

Otherwise, such as pollutin case, it can infuence inflation or deflation. Consequently, the reason indicates supply and demand theory. If air pollution is serious, then we will consider health issue, global cars demand number may be influenced to reduce, when global cars number demand will reduce, global car prices and supply number will need to change to fall down in order to attract or persuade global car consumers choose to make car purchase decision.

Hence, global car manufacture number and car price will be influenced to reduce, due to global air pollution issue. Consequently, deflation will occur because when the country citizen usually does not spend much extra saving money to buy car expensive goods. Money value will be low. Otherwise, if global cair pollution is not serious, human considers to buy cars to enjoy driving leisure lives. So, global car demand is influenced to increase , also global car price will also influenced to increase.

Consequently, gobal human will choose to buy cars to drive. Due to we accept to spend extra saving to buy expensive car goods. Car sale price and supply may be influenced to rise up. Money value is influenced to reduce. Inflation may be influenced, due to global car consumers number increases, we would not have extra money to spend easily. Car expensive goods expenditure influences our spending habit to avoid to make car purchase decision more easily. So, human intellectual or foolish activities may bring inflation or deflation consequency in possible indirectly in macro economic view.

On conclusion, above pollution case explain that how and why human intellectual or foolish economic behaviors may bring inflation or deflation consequency as wll as economic growth or recession consequency as well as any goods demand and supply increasing or decreasing consequency. It implies that human behavior may have indirect relationship to influence any goods demand and supply number to either increase or decrease result as well as any goods price will be influenced to increase or decrease in micro and macro economic view.

The relationship between social change and human behavior

Why does economic changes may influence human individual behavioral change? I shall attempt to indicate shopping behavior and staying at home behavior to explain their case and effect relationsip as below:

Human behavior can be influenced by economic change or economic change can be influenced by human behavior? Why does recession may influence consumers reduce shopping desire? In social recession suitation, it is possible that many people lose jobs suddenly, due to businessmen lose many customers. They need to make decision to reduce employees number in order to continue to keep businesses. Consequently, many firms (organizations) their employees may lose jobs. When they have much time, due to lose jobs, they will feel to avoid to spend too much time and money to go to shopping often. Many losing jobs people, they will often stay at homes. So, they will reduce time to go to shopping, then non essential products won't their preferable choice purchase products. Hence, recession will change many losing jobs people their shopping or consumption desires to avoid to buy non essential products often . Usually when economic boom, many people have jobs to do because consumers number must increase when many people have jobs to do. Then, many people can accept to spend money to buy non essential products often. Many people feel spend time to go to shopping can satisfy their purchase of any kinds of new products useful psychology or desire. So, recession is one good example to explain it can influence many people do not like often to leave homes to go to shopping easily. Many people like to stay at homes, becaue they feel worry about spending too much shopping time when they leave homes. Their staying home time is one good negative shopping behavior example. So, economic change may influence human individual behavior changes , they have direct cause and efect relationship in behavioral economic view.

May human behavior influence economic change? Is it possible that human behavior may bring the country social economic change in macro economic or micro behavioral economic view ? I shall indicate publishing industry example. Do you feel that if there are many students feel learning is very important when they read many books or many of students feel interesting to read or they have reading new books in habit, then it is possible that the country will have many students like to spend time to go to any book shops to choose the books, they feel that they can help they learn new knowledge. Then the country will increase students number, they often spend time to visit any one book shop every week. Their visiting book shops behavior which may become their habits. So, the country will increase students number, they often spend time to visit book shops. Also, it implies that visiting book shops behaviors may be their behavioral habits.

So, when the country has many students often spend time to visit book shops , their visiting book shops behaviors may help any one book shop to raise books sale chance. So, the country's student individual often visiting book shop behaviors, their habitual visiting book shops behaviors must may assist help any one book shop to increase books sale number absolutely.

Consequently, any one book shop , its books sale bumber must be influenced to increase to increase because the country will have many students like or feel need visit book shops habit in order to choose any suitable books to buy to read at home in order to raise themselves learning effort. When the country has many bok shops often have many students visit their book shops, then their books sale number may be influenced to increase. It explain why student individual visiting book shop behavior may help any one book shop sale number increases also.

How human productive behavior may influence economic development

May any country which citizen behavior assist themselves country development? It is one cause and effect economic question. I mean that if the country itself citicen can not concentrate mind or energy to choose to do one kind of industry in order to let themselves country can bring the most benefit, then whether the counry itself economy can bring the most serious economic benefit. I shall attempt to indicate these countries themselves indistry choice to explain whether these countries themselves citizen productive behavior may help themselves countries to achieve the largest economic benefits. I shall indicate as below:

New Zealand farmer individual wine productive behavior

For New Zealand country example, this country concerns itself effort is foucs on farming agricultural aspect. So, this country has many farmers concentrate on farming agricultural aspect. May New Zealanders choose to spend time to produce different kinds of wines, e.g. wine or red grape wine is for the people are eating meat, or they are eating dinner.

When these New Zealanders their behaviors choose to do farming or agriculture to grow and produce different kinds of taste of white or red grape wine drinking products job. Themselves grape agriculture behavior will influence these New Zealanders themselves, they can learn how to improve different kinds of grape wine drinking products in order to achieve every kinds of white or read grape wines taste improving aim during their white or red grape producing process.

Why can New Zealander every individual white or read grape wine producers improve their white or read grape wine taste more easily? In behavioral economic view, it can explain that why any one New Zealander white or read grape wine producer can be encouraged or excited or persuaded to concentrate nervous and energy and effort to learn how to improve their white or red grape wine products easily.

In fact, New Zealand is one agricultural food export country. It has good natural environment resource , e.g. land, seed to provide any one farmer to produce themselves any kinds of agricultrual food products, e.g. fruit, or wine food products. Because New Zealanders know themselves country has enough natural resource . So, in common, many New Zealanders choose to attempt to do farming agricultural jobs in order to export themselves any kinds of fruit or meat or wine products to overseas or sell to domestic in order to earn profit.

So, when these New Zealand farmers number has been increasing every year. This country farmers will feel themsleves competition between this New Zealand farmers themselves are serious due to they may feel New Zealanders choose to do agriculture businesses in order to export themselves different kinds of farming food to overseas or sell to local to earn profit.

Hence, when many New Zealand farmers feel that farmers number has been increasing every year. They will feel themselves competition is serious. They must need to spend much time and nervous and effort to research what method is the best how to produce the best taste of white or red grape wine products in order to let local or overseas wine buyers to choose to buy his/her producing white or read grpae products to drink.

Hence, in competition psychological view, may influence many New Zealand white or reaad wine producers had been beginning to change their learning behavior on researching what method is the best in order to produce the best quality of taste red or white wine products to sell in order to attract overseas or local white or read grape wine drinkers to choose to buy his/her wine products. Their behavior will focus on learning how to raising or improving white or read grape wine taste method more than only focus on producing a large number white or red grape wine products. They believe wine quality is more important to compare wine producing number. So, New Zealand wine producers themselves wine producers behaviors have been changing on concentrating on researching wine quality method aspect more then wine producing number aspect in behavioral economic view.

America high technological productive behavior

For America example, US is one high technological country, it owns many high technological knowledge talent inventors, e.g. computer science inventors. Hence, US must attract many diferent countries owning high technological computer inventors choose to go to US to develop their computer science profession career. Also, it seems that when many computer science inventors or professions choose to go to US to develop themselves computer science new career. In behavioral economic view, due to their leaving themselves countries choice, which may bring influence themselve country job behaviors need to be changed. They must need to adapt US new live. Because they will forgive their past computer science job. These computer science professionals need to spend time to adapt US new lives. They " past computer science job behaviors" will need to be changed to their new US any computer employer's new computer science job model.

Because their traditional computer science jobs needed to be forgot in their themselves countries. They will feel their old computer science job knowledge and behavior needed to change in order to let their US any one new of computer company employer feels satisfactory to accept their new working behavior in any one US computer organization.

So, on the other hand, many US computer company employer will feel that they must need time to accept any one new overseas computer science professions their working behaviors, their working attitude daily, because these foreign comouter science professional, their past computer working behaviors and working attitude must be different to US domestic computer science professions.

In behavioral economic view, these overseas computer science professions, their working behaviors and attitude must be needed to change in order to adapt any one US new computer company itself domestic or local computer science professional stafs themselves daily working behaviors and attitude because these overseas and local computer science professionals must need to team work together.

In behavioral economic view, it is only one way that foreign computer science professionals must need to change themselves past country traditiona daily working behaviors and attitude in order to cooperate with these US local computer science professionals in teams more easily.

Consequently, if these foreign compute science professionals can change their past working behaviors and attitude to let any one US local computer science professional feels to cooperate with them easily in short time. Then, the US computer company itself whole computer professional teams themselves efficiencies will be influenced to raised or improved by the changing past working attitude and working behaviors of these foreign computer science professionals. So, in behavioral economic view, only if US any one computer company hopes itself computer teams themselves efficiency can be raised or improved when it decides to employ foreign computer science professionals and US domestic computer science professionals. They need to work in teams together. They must need to let these foreign computer science professionals to know how to change their working behaviors and attitude to let their domestic computer science professionals feel easy to work together. Then, the US computer company itself whole team efficiency must be rasied or improved easily in short time.

● China share market investing behavior

For China share market example, economic development depends on financial market. Because if many Chinese have interest to invest to carry on shares buying and selling activities in orde to learn how to earn shares interest and share profit when the China shareholder can make decision to sell himself/herself shares in the the high price, then he/she can earn money when he/she can sell the China company's shares in the high sale share price position.

If China has many Chinese like to spend time to carry on investing shares activities. Themselves shares buying and selling behaviors will influence China has many companies can increase fund from many Chinese shareholders in order to have enough money to expand or develop themselves businesses in China in long term.

Consequently, when China can have many Chinese like to attempt to carry on buying and selling shares investing behaviors in China share market. Themselves buying and selling shares behaviors can help many Chinese companies have effort to increase enough money or capital in order to continue to do their businesses in long term absolutely. So, it explains why when many Chinese become shareholders , they can assist China will have many companies continue to develop their businesses if many Chinese like to carry on shares buying and selling investing behaviors in long time in China financial investment market nowadays in behavioral economic view.

Why has any individual country have many people invest share behavior which can influence the country's macro consumption desire?

I shall apply shares market buying and selling investment behavior to explaiin why shares investment behavior which may impact the country's overal consumption desire as below:

In behavioral economic view, I assume that when the coutry has many people have interest to attempt to carry on shares buying and selling investment behavior, then their frequent shares buying and selling behaviors which may bring negactive consumption desire or shopping desire of these shares investors their consumer behavior.

The reason is simple, when the country has many share buyers number suddenly been increasing rapidly. Consequently, these large group share investors must need to spend much time to research any kinds of company shares variations, whether when their share prices will rise up of fall down in order to achieve buying the company's shares in the lowest price and selling the company's shares in the highest price level in order to earn profit.

Basic on this reason, they must need to spend much extra time to research share prices changing behavior every day, e.g. one working person will wait to leave his/her job, after he/she can spend time to gather data to research the day's share price changing behavior after dinner. So, the working person's right time may be his/her share price market research behavior. Before he/she may spend his/her night time to go to shopping after dinner, but nowadays, he/she will fogive to do his/her shopping behavior before dinner or after dinner at hight sometime. He/she will make decision to spend much night time to turn on computer to click on share market website to research his/her share purchase choice to investigate whether his/her share price whether it rises up or falls down at the moment in order to make his/her share buying or selling decision at ever night time.

I mean the when the country has many people are share investors, their shares investment behavioral spenging time which will influence many shops lose customers at might often because the country will have many people feel need to spend night time to turn on computer or watch television to investigate share price variation. So, the country will have many people / share investors choose to stay at home in order to carry on share price variation investigation behavior, they need to listen share market update news from radios or watch the share market update news from computer or TV at home every night. Consequenly, they must reduce times to leave themselves homes at night. So, their shopping behavior also will be reduced. Because these share investors feel need to spend time to investigate share price variation news at homes which can bring economic benefits (high opportunity benefits) when they choose to forgive to leave homes to go to shopping times (opportunity cost) every night.

On conclusion, it seems that when the country has many people are share investors, then their share price investigating behavior may bring negative shopping emotion at night. Consequently, the country's any one shop may lose many customers from this share investor consumer group in behavioral economic view. Hence, when the country's share investors number had been increasing rapidly, it will influence any shops lose many customers from this share investing customer group at night frequenly in short time, even long time in behavioral economic view, because their shopping desires or shopping emotion will be brought negative feeling when they make decisions to spend much time to listen radios or watch TV or computers share price update nes at night. Hence, share market will bring negative impact to influence consumer shopping desire or negative shopping emotion in behavioral economic view.

Can technology influence human shopping behavioral change?

Nowadays, technological development has reached mature stage, whether technological mature stage may bring positive or negative shopping emotion influence to global consumers. I shall aplly internet inventin or ecommerce shopping channel tool to explain whether internet technology can bring postive or negative influence to global consumer behavior in behavioral economic view.

Internet is a good technological tool, it brings e-commerce business chance. In fact, commonly, global has have many businessmen choose to use internet channel to carry on their products transactions between global online-buyers and their electronic websites. So, global many shoppers had begun to feel online shopping is more convenient to compare visiting shops shopping. Their shopping behaviors have been changed from internet technological tool. Global has many shoppers choose to buy any products from any overseas or local businessmen their web stores. They only need to spend time to find any businessmen their webstores to choose the most suitable products to pay visa to buy from their webstores. at homes. So, in general, global had have may shoppers had changed their shopping behaviors from visiting shops to visiting webstores at homes often.

So, it seems that internet technological tool had influenced global many shops disappear, but internet webstores will be replaced their actual shops on streets. Some of businessmen either they choose webstores to replace shops or choose websotes and shops both or still keep shops only. Hence, internet tool influences global businessmen have three kinds of products sale channels to let globa local and overseas consumers to choose how to buy their products.

However, in fact, many of global shoppers, youngers and olders had begun to accept to buy any products from webstores. They feel to spend time to leave homes to visit shops , their shopping behaviors will be wasted time to not essential part to their daily lives. Hence, since internet technological invention, it had changed many consumers their traditional visiting shops shopping habit to change to buying products from webstores channel.

However, on the one hand, internet creates webstores ecommerce shopping channel to let global many consumers do not need to leave homes to go to shopping. It brings negative visiting shops shopping emotion to global general consumers nowadays. But on the other hand, it also brings positive visiting internet webstores shopping emotion to global general consumer nowadays. So, it seems that global many consumers feel that they often do not need to spend much time to go out shopping. Many global consumers feel convenient and enjoy to choose any products to buy from different internet webstores, when the online buyer chooses the most suitable product, he she only needs to pay visa card to buy the product from the online seller's webstore conveniently at home.

Hence, online shopping can bring economic benefit to online buyers, e.g. avoiding walking time or spending transport fare to visit the shop to go to shopping, shortening or reducing shopping time to do another important matter.

On conclusion, global many consumers began feel online shopping can bring more economic benefits on shortening shopping time, avoiding transport fare spending aspect. So, online shopping will be popular shopping behavior for future long time. It may encourage global many shoppers can make rapid shopping decision in short time in order to carry on any products buying transaction to global any one online shopper in short time easily in behavioral economic view. So, global many businessmen had begun to build themselves one attraction webstore in order to persuade different countries consumers to choose to click themselves webstores from internet channel to buy any kinds of products in short time easily.

So, internet technology had changed consumers traditional shopping behaviors to build positive online shopping emotion as well as raise online sellers' any products sale chance easily in behavioral economic view.

Why and how human behavior may influence the country's economic growth or recession?

When one country has many people choose to do the same matter for one period, whether their behavior may influence the country's pvera; economic growth or recession . I shall attempt to indicate cases toexplain their relationship as below:

For flowing rubblish behavioral case example, do you feel that when the country has many people often flow rubblish on the streets, instead of their flowing rubblish behavior may bring streets dirty? But, their flowing rubblish behavior may explain that this country has people may have enough money to buy food to ear, or enough cloths to wear, enough bottles of water to drink, even they may have enough money to buy new television, radio, refrigeraters , washing machines, desktops or laptops electronic home products from old to new to use in order to satisfy their living needs. So, when they flow old electronic home products, their flowing old home electronic products behaviors may seem that they have enough money to buy other new home electronic products to replace old home electronic products to use at homes.

However, it seems thaat this country ought have many people have jobs to do. So, many of them, they can easy to make purchase decison to flow any old home electronic products and buy any new home electronic products to use . Because this country has many people have jobs to do. So, they can often not use old home electonic products to become rubblishs to flow on streets after they had bought any kinds of new home electronic homes.

In fact, it also implies that this country's economy grows rapidly. So, many businesses can glow up rapdly. When they expanded their businesses, they must need to increase employees number in order to let they help themselves to raise productivity or serve their clients absolutely. So, when the country has many businesses can grow up, it seems that its economy must be better or it is improved to compare past. Due to many different kinds of home electronic products had been often bought to use by this country people in this period. So, this country's any streets can be observed that expensive electronic home products were flowed on streets anywhere. then, this country will have many electronic home products sellers can sell their home electronic products very easily. When this country has many people can find any kinds of jobs to do easily. So, due to unemploymen rate had been decreasing.

In behavioral economic view, as this many electronic home products rubblish country case, we can observe this country may have many people have jobs to do. So, consumption number has been increased long time. So, cheap food, or expensive home electronic products may be rubblish on any streets. This country's people , their flowing rubblish behaviors may be explained that many of people have enough jobs to do, so they have ability to buy any good taste food to eat or buy any kinds of expensive electronic home products to use. So, this country's economy may be improved for this long period. So, in behavioral economic view, when this country can have many electronic home products rubblishs are flowed on anywherer in streets frequently. It seems that this country will have many people have jobs to do, so it causes they often change old home electronic products or replaced them easily, when they have enough income to spend to buy any kinds of new home electronic products to use at homes easily. Moreover, their flowing old electronic home products behaviors also indicate that this country has many people their salaries may be increased in possible from their emplyers. When this country can have many different kinds of home electornic products are sold. It means that this country's electronic home products needs or demand had been increasing, due to many people have jobs to do and income increases to excite their living of needs also improve. Consequently, this country may seem have better economic improvement. We can observe from this country's electronic home products rubblish increasing income in theis period.

On conclusion, this country ought experience economic growth at this period. So, " flowing expensive electronic home rubblish increasing number " may seem that this country's economic growth is rapidly in this period, due to many people have jobs to do as well as salaries increase in this period.

Technology how impacts human behavior changing?

Technology how influences human behavior to bring changing? For example, online share purchase and sale transaction from smart phone brings share investor can do share buying or selling transation in any where and any time conveniently, non manual driving auto vehicle, bring car owner feels comfortable and spends free time to do other matter, e.g. reading, listening mucis in himself or herself car freely. electrical energy vehicle can help car owner to reduce air polluton and it can brings the drivers do not feel drive long time in any journeys in order to avoid air pollution for environmental protection responsible car drivers in our societies. Thus, they will drive long time in any journeys when they can drive electronic energy cars to replace oil energy cars.

However, online technology can also bring consumers can choose to stay at homes to buy any things from seller individual online webstore conveniently. Such as online technology can bring shoppers do not need to spend much time to visit shops to buy any things. They can choose any kinds of products from any online sellers individual online webstores conveniently at homes. Online technology excite busy consumers can make purchase decision easily as well as it can help online sellers sell any kinds of products from internet easily.

In behavioral economic view, technology can change human behavior to be improved, it can let human feels comfortable, more free time ro use, rapid making any decisions, such as apply smart phones to make share purchase or sale transaction decision, online shopping decision, even travelling any where decision in short time, when the traveller finds the most cheap hotel accommodation room price and air ticket price frm any travel agent online tourism webstore, then the potential travel customer can follow the online hotel accommodation price and air ticket price data to make decision when to buy the air ticket from the airline travel agent or make decision when to prebook which hotel accommodation room to go to the country to travel from online travel agent tourism webstores. So, technology can encourage global any country travelers to make anywhere to trvel rapidly. If the traveler can find the country's general hotel rooms and airline tickets prices had been decreasing more sightly. The traveler may make travel decision to choose the country to travel in short time, then he/she can prebook the country;s any hotel room and airline ticket to pay by visa fraom the country's any hotel and airline travel agent webstores., before one week, even one month or more easily. Hence, online technology can also encourage traveler individual frequent travel times to be increased, due to global travelers can find any hotel rooms and airline tickets prices from internet conveniently at homes. They do not need to spend time to visit any airline travel agent to enquire travel choice country's hotel rooms prices and airline ticket prices. They can compare global travel of countries choices ' all hotels rooms and airline agents air tickets prices to make prebook airline seat and hotel room decision before one week, one month even six months early.

On conclusion, online technology can encourage global travelers can make travelling any where and when traveling time desicions easily. It can excite tourism industry develops in long time. Also, such as electricity cars invention can encourage environment protection car owners do car purchase decision easily, because they can choose to drive electronic energy cars to replace oil energy cars in order to avoid air pollution occurs easily. So, electronic cars can increase electronic car purchasrs number, due to many of environmental protection attitude of car owners can choose to drive electricity cars to bring air cleans, even non -manual driving cars can encourage lazy driving and free time driving car owners to choose to buy non-manual (artificial intelligent) cars to drive , because they can spend much free time to read, listen music or do any matters in themselves cars, they do not need to drive cars, robotic (AI) auto driving machine is such one non-manual driver to help them to drive themselves cars confidently. So, non-manual driving cars can attract lazy and enjoying free time driving car owners to choose to buy to replace traditional manual cars to drive easily. Moreover, online share transaction can help any share investors to make share buying and selling decision in short time easily. When they can apply smart phones technological tool to carry on share buying and selling activities easily. They can observe any share rising or falling price suitation from smart phones in any where any any time easily. So, smart phone technology can help global any shareholders to make share purchase and sale transaction easily. So, technology can encourage human makes decision in short time rapidly.

How and why employees behaviors may influence economy development?

In behavioral economy view,I believe the country's any organizational employees behavior may bring indirect relationship to influence the country's long term economic development. I shall indicate past manufacture industry social development period to explain their relationship. For many countries' past business activities had belonged to manufacturing industry, such as US, UK past before 1980 year, it focused on steel manufacturing and steel manufacturing related machine products. So, US, Uk developed countries manufacturing industries may be past main country's economic income sources. I assume US , UK past had one million number different kinds of industries. They ought had about seven houndred thousand number organizational businesses were belonged to manufactured industry. They may include:
Steel manufacturing and steel related machine manufacturing, e.g. vehicle manufacturing, home appliances, e.g. washing machine, television, radio, refrigerate cooler, heater, air condition etc. different kinds of different kinds of steel -related manufacturing machine, they were manufactured from US, UK steel machine manufacturers. So, US, Uk the other three hundred thousand number industry may be general service industry, e.g. hotel service, restaurent, cinema, public transport service, tourism lesiure , wine bar, supermarket etc. different kinds of non-manufacturing industries business organizations were operated in UK, US past before 1980 year.
So, in UK, US developed countries industry development history, they ought have high percentage of businesses belonged to steel related manufacturing machine and steel products. Also, in the past before 1980 year, US, Uk business employers , they employed many workers are manufacturing workers. They needed to spend long time to work in factories. They were skillful workers, and they are trained to manufacturing cars, washing machine, television, heater, etc. even steel itself different kinds of steel related products to prepare to deliver to their shops to sell to US, Uk local or overseas clients.
So, I believe that past UK, US ought employ many employees, they belonged to skillful manufacturing workers, manufacture increasing steel machine or

steel related machine number of products rapidly daily. So, if UK, US had had many of these manufacturing factories owned high skillful workers, then their manufacturing steel-related machine or steel both kinds of products number must be influenced to raise rapidly. Consequently, their steel machine manufacturing products would been exported to overseas or would been sold to local both markets , they may be influenced to raise sale number. They (these manufacturing workers) needed to be trained to know how to manufactur these different kinds of machine products in the efficient teams and they ought to be trained to raise their efficiencies in order to shorten time to manufacturing many kinds of steel related manufacturing machine or steel itself products rapidly. So , if their efficiencies and manufacturing performance was improved, these US, UK any one manufacturing worker and their teams ought achieve raising productivities significantly.

Hence, when past UK, US manufacturing industry development period, if these two countries' any manufacturing factories could have many manufacturing workers could be trained to be skillful and proficient manufacturing workers. Then, in past every day to these factories workers, they ought help their steel or steel related manufacturing employers to raise any kinds of machine or steel products number in every team. So, when past in the manufacturing industry development, US, UK could have many factories' manufacturing workers themselves steel or steel related machine products manufacturing skill could be trained to to improve to any kinds of these machine or steel manufacuring products quality as well as their products number could be influenced to raise by themselves skillful improvement significantly every day.

Then, what would be influenced to occur to past UK, US manufacturing industry period? In behavioral economic view, when these two manufacturing industry developed countries, such as UK, US , if they had many factories workers can be trained to improve their skill in order to achieve any kinds of steel or steel-related machine products quality could be improved as well as products manufacturing number could be also increased absolutely.

In consequence, past UK and US both countries ought increase themselves any kinds of steel and steel related machine products number to be supplied to themselves local shops to let local clients to choose any one kind of machine manufacturing products to buy easily as well as they could also export to supply overseas any countries to buy their different kinds of steel or steel related machine products to let overseas steel or steel related manufacturing machine product buyers, they can have many of these different kinds of these steel or steel-related different kinds of manufacturing machine from UK and UK these both countries easily to compare other countries.

On conclusion, I believe that past US, and UK macro manufacturing industry income GDP would increase significantly. So, they would have good economic growth performance because when many of these manufacturing workers themselves manufacturing effort could be improved. So, it explained when employees manufacturing abilities can influence economic growth indirectly.

Robots invention whether they can help organizations to raise efficiencies or inefficiencies?

In behavioral economic view, in any organizations, when the organization hopes its worker teams can raise efficiencies , the organization may choose to increase more workers number and/or it can provide training to improve these workets themselves skills in order to raise their efficiencies. For one warehouse example, when the warehouse increases many goods , they are needed to delivered these goods from the shelves to the delivering destination locations. If this warehouse supervisors feel these workers themselves goods delivery speeds are slow, which is possible due to this warehouse's workers number is not enough. So, this warehouse supervisor ought increase workers number in order to increase their goods delivery speed in order to deliver goods from the shelves to every indicated goods delivery destination in order to let any one lorry driver can transport the right kinds of goods and ensure the accurate goods number to transport to any one client home rapidly.

However, if this warehouse supervisor planed to buy several warehouse goods delivery robots to assist these warehouse workers to find the right kinds of goods from shelves and then deliver to the right destination location in the warehouse. So, these warehouse orkers can concentrate on counting the accurate goods number and ensuring the right kinds of goods in order to prepare to let lorry drivers to transport these goods to these goods of buyers themselvers homes rapidly. Consequently, in the first step, robots can concentrate on finding th right goods from shelves and delivers them to the right goods transportation of location destination. Then, in the second step, these warehouse workers can concentrate on counting the accurate goods number and ensuring the right kinds of goods in order to prepare to put them to the lorry. Consequently, when warehouse robots and warehouse workers can cooperate to work together, the most important, robots, can deal on finding the right kinds of goods and deal on delivering the accurate number of goods of job duty as well as these warehouse workers can only concentrte on counting the right kinds of goods number in order to avoid it has none any mistake of wrong kinds of goods and inaccurate goods of delivery number to be transported to the lorry and to deliver to any one buyer's home.

So, it seems that warehouse robots ought help any one warehouse worker to raise himself efficiency and avoid goods delivery of mistake occurrence easily as well as their help to warehouse workers that can let any one goods buyer feels their goods can be delivered to their homes rapidly. Moreover, warehouse robots can also help these warehouse workers to raise efficiencies because warehouse robots can help them to shorten goods delivery time between any one shelf and any one goods delivery destination of location in the warehuse because robots may help them to find the right kinds of goods from the right shelf in the short time. So, any one worker does not need to spend long time to seek anywhere is the right shelf location for the kind of goods when the kind of goods are needed to deliver to the buyer's home from lorry. Warehouse robots can help them to do this aspect of " finding the goods from the right shelf in short time job duty". So, any one warehouse worker only needed tospend less time to do the counting of any right kind of goods number and ensuring the right kind of goods job duty. Consequently, this warehouse 's any one worker, his any one kind of goods delivery time may be reduced, because robots' assistance and they may have more confidence to avoid mistake to deliver the wrong number of goods and/or the wrong kind of goods to any one goods buyer's home.

On conclusion, it seems that warehouse robots ought may help any one warehouse worker to raise efficiency for any one team in the warehouse as well as the warehouse any one supervisor does not need to spend much time to observe any one worker individual performance for " goods delivery job duty aspect" because their goods delivery job duty that had been replaced to do by these several warehouse robots. Robots can achieve the more accurate of right kinds of goods and the right number of goods delviery job performance to compare any one of human warehouse worker themselves right kinds of goods of delivery and right number of goods of delivery job performance. So, when robots can participate to cooperate with this warehouse's any one worker to do their goods of delivery job duty in this warehouse every day. Then, robots can raies any one of supervisor individual confidence in order to let they do not need to spend time to observe any one of worker individual whose goods of delivery job performane. They can concentrate on supervising any one worker whose goods transport to lorry in the final step in order to avoid to deliver wrong goods number and / or wrong kind of goods to any one goods buyer's home every day. Consequently, this warehouse's overall teams of their delviery of goods performance many be improved by robotss' participatin to goods of delivery task as well as this warehouse's oveall teams themselves efficiencies may be influenced to raise by robots' goods of delivery task participation.

Why social behavior may influence organizational strategy needs to be changed ?

Why any organizations need to know whether nowadays social behaivor how has been changing in order to implement the kind of the most right strategy to achieve the profit aim pursue in possible. I shall indicate nowadays ecommerce or online, customer shopping behavior to explain above question concerns they ought have close relationship between social behavior and organizational strategic choice or organizational behavioral changing need.

On nowadays ecommerce business, or online shopping model, this kind of shopping model in global many young and old age consumers like to apply internet tool to choose any country sellers website stores in order to stay at home to buy any kinds of products from themselves webstores in global societies.

In fact, online shopping model had been popular for long time above to twenty years. Most of global sellers will make decision to design themselves webstores in order to attract global many online buyers to choose to buy their products from themselves webstores. So, it seems that social consumers purchase behaviors had been changed to online shopping from internet invention.

Hence, social consumers purchase behavioral changes may influence any organizations' strategies need to be changed from visiting shops purchase strategy model to online purchase strategy model, if the seller still concentrate on concentrate on considerate how to design itelf , but neglects to considerate how to design itself webstore, e.g. how to design attract product photos to put on itself webstore, how to arrange sale price information location to be putted on webstore and visa card payment location on itself webstore in order to let any one online buyer can feel very easier to buy itself any kinds of products from itself webstore. Then, its potential online buyers will be influenced to increase number when they can find this online seller itself any kinds of products photes and every kinds of product sale price information and visa card payment channel locations easily from itself webstore.

So, it implies that nowadays any one seller ought need to design one webstore to let any one online overseas and domestic consumers can have chance to click itself webstore to choose any one kind of product to buy conveniently when he/she does not hope to leave him/her home to go to shop, because nowadays social shopping behaviors had been influenced to change when internet invention, them it gives another online purchase method to replace visiting shops purchase method to global any one buyer in nowadays societies.

So, if nowadays any one seller still concentrate on how to design itself shop display in order to put any kinds of product on shelf in order to let any one visiting shop customer to find the kind of product to buy, but it neglects to change to choose to pursue another new technological shopping method, such as webstore purchase method in order to implement effective strategy to design the most right webstore as well as in order to attract global overseas and local consumers to find itself webstore easily from website and find its any one kind of product phots and sale price and visa card payment button in order to choose to buy itself any kinds of products in the short time. Consequently I believe that the seller will lose many customers from overseas and local when its other same or similar product sellers choose to design themselves webstores in order to let global any one product buyer can buy themselves any one kind of product when they can pay visa card to buy their products from them webstores conveniently when they stay at home habitly. Then, the seller will lose many global potential customers in long time.

On conclusion, in behavioral economic view, any consumer behavioral social changing, which will influence any in order to avoid customers number loses significantly . In future time, organizations need to make rapid decision in order to implement the most reasonable and the most useful strategy in order to avoid global potential customers number reduces or lose them in long time. So, social behavioral changing environment ought influence any global organizations need to decide how to change themselves strategies in order to avoid customers loses significantly in future time.

How and why human behavior may influence economic growth or recession?

May ourselves daily behaviors influence our global societial continue economic growth or recession? Do they have cause and effect close relationship between human behaviors and global economic growth or recession? I shall apply behavioral economic theory to analyze and explain whether ourselves daily behaviors and our global societial economic growth or recession which have close cause and effect relationship as below:

Every country itself economic development must depend on any business activities, otherwise, any kinds of business activities must need ourselves business activities or behaviors in order to achieve any business activities as well as achieve the country's overall economic development in macro view. However, any country's overall business activites or behaviors which must depend on any kinds of individual businessmen, themselves employees daily working behavior or activity or performance in order to help them to attract or increase many clients number to acieve " earning profit" aim. So, it seems that any individual business, itself overall every department individual working behavior is one main factor to influence the company's overall business performance.

For agricultural fruit and meat food farming industry example, such as New Zealand is a farming main target industry country. It had had many New Zealanders were daily themselves own farming businesses for many years. Their farming businesses include growing fruit, sheep, cow, pig pork, meat etc. food sale business. If the New Zealand farmer owned a large size farming land, then he will choose either growing fruit or feeding sheeps, pigs, cows to be meat to to transport to New Zealand supermarkets to help them to sell to their farmers meet to New Zealanders in order to earn profit. Thus, if the New Zealand farmer owned large size of farming lands, then he needs to employ many farming employees (farming workers) to help him to carry on farming business daily tasks, e.g. picking up friuts, feeding pigs, cows, sheeps to eat food daily. These daily farming jobs are very important to influence this New Zealand farmer's meats or fruits sale number whether they can be easy or diffcult to sell in New Zealand supermarkets , if these farming workers can own encough farming knowledge or skill to know how to pick up fruits method and make judgement to know whether it is right time to pick up the kind of fruits from the trees , as well as know how feed this pigs, sheeps, cows to eat food in order to let they are better health. Consequently, their farming behaviors which can let these animals can provide the best taste and enough meat from these animals to let New Zealander to buy to eat from New Zealand any one supermarket. Even these New Zealand farming workers can know whether the kinds of fruits, e.g. oranges, apples, gapes etc. fruits whether they ought be picked up from the trees at the right time. Consequently, they can make judgement to decide to pick up any kinds of the best taste fruits to let any one New Zealander to buy to eat from any one supermarket in New Zealand. Otherwise, if they do not make judegement to know whether the kind of fruit ought not be picked up because they still need longer time to continue grow up to increase fruit size and better taste from the trees in order to let any one fruit buyer can feel better taste when they eat this kind of fruit later. If they can buy this kind of fruit to eat later, then this New Zealand farmer's his fruit buyers can buy the best taste of this kind of fruit to eat from an yone supermarket in New Zealand. Consequently, many New Zealand supermarkets will choose to buy any kinds of fruits from this farmer fruit supplier when they feel this farmer's fruits can provide more better taste fruits to compare other farmers' fruits.

Thus, due to New Zealand is one farming main income source country. It's any kinds of fruits and meats need to be export to overseas to sell , instead of local sale. It's GDP percent is very high to whole country 's overall income source. So, any one New Zealand farmer individual and any one farming worker individual working behavior will influence its economy whether it is influenced to grow or recession possible. Moreover, it also seems that farming workers' farming knowledge and skill will influence themselves farming daily activities to achieve the aim of the number of increase or decrease to any kinds of fruits whether they are better taste or the number of increase of decrease to any kinds of meats whether they are better taste to supply to any one New Zealand fruit or meat buyers to eat from any one New Zealand supermarket. So, it implies that any one New Zealand farming worker individual farming behavior may influence any kinds of fruits or any kinds of meat taste because they are transported to any one supermarket to sell in New Zealand.

Consequently, if New Zealans had many farmers can teach god farming knowledge and skill to let their any one farming workers know how to decide judgement to decide when it is right time to pick up any kinds of fruits from trees , or how to grow them on soil in order to let they can grow rapidly. Then, many different kinds of fruits can be provided to let any one New Zealanders can eat the best taste of fruits when their fruits are supplied to any one New Zealand supermarkets. Even, if they knew how to feed foods to pigs, cows, sheeps to eat daily. Then they can be more health and they can provide the best taste of meats to let any one New Zealanders can buy their meats from any one New Zealand supermarkets. Moreover, their fruits and meats can be transported to overseas to let any one country fruits or meats buyers can choose any kinds of New Zealand meats and fruits to buy to eat from themselves countries supermarkets. Then, many overseas fruit and meat buyers will perfer to choose New Zealand any kinds of fruits or meats to buy to compare other countries fruits or meats to buy when they go to any one local supermarkets.

On conclusion, it seems that New Zealand farming workers themselves farming behavior may influence their farming employers any kinds of fruits or meats sale number and income because their farming task behaviors must influence whether their fruits or meats taste are the better taste or worse taste to compare their other local farmers (the farmer competitors) whose fruits or meats taste. If tthe farmer's any one farming worker can be trained to learn how to know to feed animals skill and when is the most right time to pick up any kinds of fruits from trees or how to grow them on the soil methods. Due to these farming worker individual farming behavior may influence his different finds of fruits and meats sale number to be increase or decrease, so these any one New Zealand farmer must need to depend on any one farming worker whose farming working methods, if their farming working behaviors can be the best to influence any kinds of fruits to grow rapid or any kinds of pigs, cows, sheeps animals grow up rapidly , then their sale number may be increase significantly and their taste can be improved to let any New Zealand or overseas meat or fruit buyer to buy to eat to feel from any one New Zealand or overseas supermarkets, then New Zealand's agriculture industry must be influenced to increase. In the world, any one fruit or meat buyer must choose to buy New Zealand's fruit and meat to eat in prefer to compare other countries' fruits and meats. So, New Zealand's GDP may be influenced to raise from any one New Zealand farming worker individual farming working behaviors.

Reasons why human behavior may influence economic recession or growth?

Can ourselves daily behaviors or activies influence ourselves countries' economic growth or recession? I shall attempt to explain the reasons why they have direct or indirect relationship between human behavior and economy growth or recession as below:

I shall indicate environment pollution case to attempt to explain above question. Our societies had been experiencing servious environment pollution challenge. However, environment pollution , such as air pollution is caused by air planes and vehicles emission by air planes and vehicles emission as well as water pollution is caused by plastic rubblish, or dirty water or oil or gas chemical material, these both kinds of pollution ought may bring economic recession and this both kinds of pollution are caused by human ourselves daily foolish activities.

I believe human behavior and economy and pollution which have cause and effect relationship. I shall analyze this environment pollution case to explain why they have case and effect relationship between human foolish behavior and environment pollution and economic recession as below:

When global societies had many people like to buy cars to drive to bring emission to fresh air on the roads as well as many manufacturing factories will bring emission to pollute fresh air in their manufacturing processes. Factories and cars will bring air pollution , due to factories need to pollute fresh air in order to manufacture many products and car owners need to drive their cars to go to offices or leisure places. Their cars will also bring emisson to pollute fresh air. On consequence, car owners themselves frequent driving behaviors and factory workers themselves frequent manufacturing behaviors may bring environment pollution. Technology or human behavior whether may influence economic growth or recession. Moreover, air planes also brings emission to pollute air when they are flying in sky. Also, when ships bring oil pollution or sea plastic rubblishs bring pollution to global oceans.

In fact, manufactuers and cars owners, such as factories workers manufacturing behaviours ans car owners driving behaviors and pilots driving air planes flying behaviors and ships transport behaviors, which may cause plastic rubblish, oil or gas emission to sky or sea or on the road to cause ocean and air pollution is serious. However, human ourselves need to buy cars to drive to satisfy ourselves driving leisure or enjoyment, travelers need to catch air planes to travel to enjoy leisure needs, factories workers need help factories to manufacture many products to sell to customers to satisfy their using needs. oil exploration needs to find lands to explore new oil lands.

All of these business and leisure activites may bring serious air and water pollution. However, due to serious air and water pollution will bring earth warming challenge , such as some countries temperature will be influences to rise up to 40 degree or higher br earth warming. However, earth warming is caused by air and ocean pollution. Pollution must be caused by human ourselves, driving cars leisure and factories manufacturing business activities. Hence, if human decided to continue to do these foolish behaviors, we only pursue to manufacture different kinds of industrial products or drive cars to enjoy leisure aims, but we also neglect ourselves behaviors may bring environment pollution. Then, earth warming or earth temperature will be influenced to rise up absolutely in long term. Moreover, if our future earth will be influenced to bring serious high temperature effect by human ourselves these foolish behaviors.

On consequencey, warth warming will bring serious economic losses in possible because when ourselves earth temperature had been influenced to rise up to 40 degree or high. Ourselves health will be caused poor, due to we will feel difficult breath, we must need often tried and hard to work, due to our nervous and health will be influenced to poor by pollution and earth warming effect. Also, we need to pay more money to see doctors when we had long life. Then, our societies will lose may strong labors to help manufacturers to work, e.g. factories will reduce workers number to help manufacturers to produce more different kinds of products, due to workers health is general poor. Due to lacking enough workers to manufacture products, our societies will begin to reduce enough supply number of products to sell to global consumers to satisfy their use needs.

On conclusion, in behaviroal economic view, our societies will lose many labors due to their bodies are not health by air and water pollution. Global economic and business activities will be influenced to worse by global workers reducing number reason. So, economic recession will begin to occur in possible when pollution reaches the serious level.

How employee behavior influences organizational development?

Can any organizational department employee individual behavior may help the organization to bring long term development? When one employee individual behavior, manager won't feel whose task behavior may help organizational development, but when the department has many teams cooperate to work together , all of these team employees whose task behaviors may help their organization to bring long term development.

I shall explain how any why when the organization has many departments, as well as when every team memmber individual behavior may help whole organization to bring long term development in possible as below:

Every organization must need efficient department to cooperate to work together. They may include human resource, finance, logistic, facility management, sales, marketing , operateional , warehouse , factory manufacture , research and development, purchase, customer service etc. different kinds of departments to cooperate to work together. So, any one employee individual behavior, include manager, leader, supervisor, worker, salesperson, manufacture worker, adminisration staff, factory or logistic worker etc. themselves task behavior whether his/her performance is worse or better , whose task behavior ought bring long term good or bad influence to cause the organization's whose efficiency, or performance , whether it can be influenced to improve significantly. For car factory manufacture workers department example, it exmploys 100 car manufacturing workers. They need to manufacture at least 50 cars in order to bring enough car manufacture number to supply to global car buyers to choose to buy (satisfaction to car buyers their driving leisure activity needs). However, if this car manufacture firm employs many low skilful car manufacture workers, their inefficient car skill may bring cars manufacture number reduces, they can not achieve to reach the at least 50 cars manufacture number, if these 100 car manufacture workers. They have half number of workers, they only manufacture 30 to 40 cars number at least daily. So, it seems that this car manufacture firm will have half car manufacture workers bring the low cars manufacture number to compare the another half cars manufacture workers, when this proficient car manufacture workers may manufacture at least 60 or more cars manufacture number daily. So, it explains that this inefficient car manufacture workers will not help this car manufacture company to manufacture enough cars number in order to supply to global car market to sell to satisfy global car buyers needs, when car buyers demand number is more thn car manufacture supply number in supply and demand view. Hence, in long term, if this car manufacture company can not employ new proficient car manufacture workers to replace those inefficient or low skillful car workers. Consequently, its car manufacture number must be influenced to reduce and it can not satisfy global car buyers driving leisure needs.

However, if this car manufacture firm also has shop to sell itself any kinds of cars, instead of manufacturing cars product. So, it needs have both main departments to help it to earn profit. The first step, it needs have proficient car manufacture workers to help it to manufacture at least 50 cars from every car worker in order to have enough cars number to be provided to global car sellers to help it to sell to global car customers. Second step, if it decided to attempt to sell itself cars. Then, it needs to set up car shops in global to different countries in order to let global car buyers may visit its global any one car shop to enquire any one car etc. salesperson about any car quality, speed, gas useful, price, safety, etc. information questions and they can attempt to sit in any one car to feel whether which car can let them to feel more comfortable to make final car purchase decision in any one shop. So, if this car company can provide good sale speaking skillful training to any one car salesperson to let his/her to know whether how to explain every kind of car function and feature, manufacture method etc. questions, then I believe that they can influence any one car buyer to makecar purchase choice decision more easily. So, it this car manufacturer hopes it may attempt to earn profit from different countries car sellers and car buyers both. It ought also provide training course to all general car salespeople to be proficient owning sale speaking skillful professional skill in order to prepare having more confidence to persuade any one car customer to make car purchase choice from any one car salesperson more easily to compare global other car sellers.

Hence, if this car manufacturer could build both car manufacturing team and car sale team more proficient. However, if this car manufacturer hopes to develop itself car manufacture busness to expend to car sale business both in success. It must need to spend long term to provide training courses to general car manufacture workers and general car salespeople both to be proficient car skillful manufacture workers and proficient car skillful salespeople in order to help they can manufacture enough car numbers and help they can persuade may car customers can make car purchase decision in short time when they visit its any one car shop.

However, this car manufacture company explains why every car manufacture worker whose manufacturing behavior and every car salesperson sale persuading speaking ability may help this car manufacture company to expand from its car manufacture market to car sale market development in sussess in possible. So, this car manufacture firm must need these two kinds of essential human resource elements in order to achieve its cars sale number and cars manufacture number increasing aim. They may include proficient car manufacture workers and proficient car salespeople both human resource elements. These both human resource daily task behavior may influence its long term task efficient performance in order to expand itself car sale business in success from itself car manufacture business easily. If it hopes to expand its car manufacture business to car sale business in success. It must need to provide training to these two departments general staffs to be proficient staffs in order to supply enough cars number to its global car shops to let global car buyers can choose its any kinds of cars to buy in any time.

Morevoer, if this car manufacture company can have good skillful of car research and development department , it aims to research and innovate any new technological cars invention in order to improve its any traditional old kinds of cars to be innovative new kinds of cars from every year. Consequently, its any new innovative cars ought attract global any one car buyer to make car purchase choice final decision more easily, because its any kinds of manufacturng cars can be innovated rapidly to compare its any one car manufacturing competitors, when its nay kinds of cars can be shorten time to innovate within three months, but its any one car manufacturing competitors need to spend more than three months, even one year to innovate themselves traditional old cars products in long term. Hence, its car staffs research and development department staffs must need own good car product design ability, proficient car engineering knowledge , even car invention knowledge in order to innovate its any one kind of car product in short time and introduce to let its global car proficient car buyers feel surprise to its any one kind of innovative car products to compare its any one car manufacturer.Hence, these four departments: car manufacture, car sale and car research and development anr car training departments must need concentrate resource to provide enough training to any one staffs in order to achieve the best performance.

On conclusion, all these departments staffs their performance can influence car manufacture aim to chance to car manufacture and sale aim more significantly. it explains why some main department staffs whole behaviors may influence any organizational performance significantly.

Artificial intelligent Human clever and art creating ability methods

How robots create human clever and art creating ability? Nowadays robots invention may help businesses to reduce employees number, improve performance, raise productivities, reduce cost in service industry,manufacturing industry, office , warehouse, restaurant, hotel , factory, cinema etc. different kinds of business environments, even public transport tools. However, instead of robots may bring these above advantages to any kinds of business working and service environments, whether robots may also help human to create clever and image creating ability. I shall attempt to answer this question:

On the one hand, I believe that past technology ,e.g. machine , it should not have ability to help human to create clever and image creative ability,but nowadays, robots invention that I believe it had had enough ability to help future human to raise more clever and more creating image or painting picture, art design etr. image ability, after robots had been experienced above more than ten years improvement stage from early research stage to invention stage, till to nowadays improvement stage, e.g. non-manual driving auto vehicels, even future non-manual driving skill may be improved to apply to public transport tools, e.g. trams, trains,buses, airplanes, ships etc. public transport tools, when non-manual driving skills can be improved to own the most safe driving skillful ability to compare human driving skills.

On another hand, when robots could be invented to be applied to medical or hospital surgery aspect, e.g. roboting surgerys may help surgery doctors to do complex surgery in surgery rooms, or serving patients tasks in any hospital working environments. They can help nurses and doctors to spend more time to do more important tasks urgently, so medical or surgery serving robots may help nurses and surgery doctors to reduce task load pressure and create clever or improve their surgery skills to when they can cooperate to work in hospitals.

On the other hand, robots can be invented to help any public transport drivers to avoid more traffic accidents occurrence on any countries roads. So, it seems that non-manual driving public transport tools invention may also help human drivers to improve driving skills in possible, when they can learn how to avoid sudden traffic accidents occurrence in any countries roads in any time. so, any kindsof public transport tool drivers ought learn how to avoid traffic accidents skills from future non-manual driving robots invention. Instead of non-manual driving robots and hospital patients medical care or surgery service robots may help public transport tools drivers and hospital nurses and doctors to concentrate on spending time to treat any more important and urgent matters every days. Even, future restaurants may let cooking restaurants may let cooking robots to help human cookers to cook more different kinds of good taste food, to human cookers may learn cooking robots cooking skills in order to improve themselves traditional cooking skills often, in order to compare their cooking skills between human cookers and cooking robots.

On conclusion, it seems that cooking robots ought help human cookers to create any kinds of new cooking skills. Moremove, futuer robot cookers ought be future human cookers their cooking coaches. These robot cookers will help human cookers to create clever cooking skills in possible. Also, future non-manual driving robots ought help human drivers to create new driving skills in order to improve their driving skills to reduce sudden traffic accidents occurrence easily on any countries roads in any time, future hospital surgery or patient care service robots may help surgeons or nurses to do any surgerys in surgery rooms or looking care patients in hospitals. So, when robot surgeons help human surgeons to do complex surgerys in surgerical rooms, human surgeons can learn how to do more complex surgerical tasks for every surgeons when human surgeons can observate every surgerical robots how to do surgeons together. Hence, it seems that robot surgeons also may create future human surgeons themselves innovate surgerical skills from traditional surgerical skills improvement. So, future artificial intelligent technology ought help any kinds of human occupations to create clever, even improvement themselves traditional skills to new innovative skills absolutely.

Why does technology raise online products sale demand and reduces shops products sale demand?

Nowadays robot technology is popular to be applied to different aspects of our daily lives. They may include: non-manual driving vehicles, smart phones, space rockets, kitchen cookers, shopping centres service, cinema ticket sale, etc. different kinds of businesses demand. However, instead of internet invention may influence global communication, media channel is changed to computer internet, media channel is changed to computer internet, media communication from traditional newspaper, letter, TV, radio etc. communication channel. So, any internet users may click to yahoo.com news website to read global news from computer yahoo.com website easily.

In fact, internet technology is also used from businesses. They attempt to set up themselves web stores to sell their products from themselves webstores. So, any one product buyers may buy any kinds of products from any one webstores when they stay at homes. It is very convenient and common to future any one webstore shoppers. It brings this question: Can webstores help online product purchases needs raise and influence shop product purchases need reduce?

In demand and supply view, when one product price raises, its sale demand ought reduce, unless, it can attract to influence customers need consideration or its supply number decreases. But, when one product is increasing sale price to seel from the seller's webstore, whether its sale number will be influenced to reduce. Also, when the kind of product is selling and its sale price is raised, whether it can still keep demand number increase as well as whether it can influence its similar kinds of competitor their products sale demand number to reduce from shop sale channel.

In demand and supply view, when one product price raises, its sale demand ought reduce, unless, it can attract to influence customers need consideration or its supply number decreases. But when one product is increasing sale price to sell from the seller's webstore, whether its sale number will be influenced to reduce. Also, when the kind of product is selling and its sale price is raised, whether it can still keep demand number increases as well as whether it can influence its similar kinds of competitors their products sale demand number to reduce from shop sale channel.

I suppose that webstore sale may influence shop sale demand number decreases, because when internet is popular to use, when one country's buyer wants to buy one kind of product, but he/she can not find the kind of product can be bought from himself/herself home country. If he/she can findthe kind of product to buy from any one of overseas webstore from internet channel at home in any time. Then, he/she will be influenced to make purchase decision from the seller's websote immediately. So, it implies that when on consumer plans to buy one kind of product, he / she will attempt to find the kind of product from any one seller's webstore in preferat home, if he/she spend long time to find the kind of product from many of webstores, but he /she still does not find the kind of product from many of webstores, then he/she will choose to visit any one shop to attempt to buy the kind of product.Hence, online shopping purchase channel will be prefer choice to compare visiting shopd purchase channel in nowadays society.

So, it explains that why the kind of product online sale number may influence the kind of similar product visiting shop sale number either increases or decreases. It means that the kind of product visiting shops sale number may still increases , if the kind of similar products supply number is not enough , they are difficult to let any one online buyer to find to buy from any one webstore. Otherwise, if the kind of similar products sale supply number is enough to let any one online buyer to find from many webstores. Then, they can influence the similar kinds of shop products purchase demand to reduce and their shops purchase demand will be also influenced to reduce from webstores purchase channel.

On conclusion, it explains that the kind of shop products demand number ought be influenced to increase or decrease, when the similar kind of products can be bought easily from many webstores from internet (e-commerce) shopping channel. Internet (online) technology may help the seller to raise the kind of product competitive ability on purchase demand aspect, when there are not many other sellers can provide webstores to sell the similar kind of products and they only concentrate on selling the kind of similar products from shops to let any one online buyer to frind from may webstores. Then, they can influence the similar kinds of shop products purchase demand to reduce and their shops purchase demand will be also influenced to reduce from webstores purchase channel. Hence, webstore and shop both purchase channel explains that the similar kinds of shop products demand number will be influenced to increase or decrease , when the kinds of product can be bought easily from many webstores from internet shopping channel. Internet technology may help the seller to raise the kind of product competitive abilty to raise purchase demand when there are not many other sellers can provide webstores to sell the kind of similar products and they only concentrate on selling the kind of similar products from shops.

Does car technological development reach mature stage to help economic development?

Our societies had been developing too many years. In our past technological aspect, machine invention had began till to computer invention till to internet invention. It seems that our technological development stage may reach mature stage. Why do I feel our technological development had reached mature stage. I shall apply demand and supply economic theory to explain this question as below:

I shall indicate car development industry to explain whether when car development stage can reach mature stage, it may help global economic growth. In our car technological development stage, it is from gas energy car invention till to nowadays battery energy car invention till to even future non-manual driving car invention. Do you feel that when human (car buyers) felt environmental protecion need to avoid air pollution. So, battery energy cars demand number may increase , it will influence gas energy cars demand number reduces. Even, if future non0manula driving cars invention succeed, lazy driving car buyers will choose to buy non-manual driving (robot driving cars) in preference. So, it is possible that , it will influence future gas energy cars demand number reduces much. I mean that when car buyers can choose many different kinds of non-manual driving cars and battery energy cars to buy. Then, gas energy cars demand number must be influenced to reduce very much as well as gas energy cars supply number will be influenced to reduce to avoid sale prices reduce.

Hence, it explains why future car technological development will reach mature stage when both kinds of non-manual driving cars and battery energy cars are invented to the mature stage. When these two kinds of cars invention can satisfy future global car buyers driving needs. Then, car maufacturers won't need to spend too much time to continue to attempt to invent any new kinds of cars in order to excite future car buyers' purchase decision. So, I believe that car technological development will reach mature stage within five years, if non-manual driving cars and battery energy cars are invented in success and they can be popular to accept to drive to global car buyers.

On conclusion, when car technological development reaches matural stage, it will help future economy continue grows because when car manufacturers had invented many new kinds of non-manual driving cars and new kinds of non-manual driving cars and new battery energy car sale market. Then, they will encourage or attract global many car buyers choose to buy these both kinds of cars products in preference to compare to traditional gas energy car products. So, they will influence many traditional gas- energy car buyers forgive to drive gas energy cars to avoid non pollution and lazy driving behavioral feeling. So, gas energy car reselling number will increase between gas energy car drivers and past non-owning any car buyers. Also, non-manual driving cars and battery energy car supplying number will be influenced to increase when battery energy car buyers and non-manual driving car buyers driving needs increase.

Consequently, these factors will influence global gas energy cars, non-manual driving cars and battery energy cars their cars purchase and sale transactions increase in future global car market. So, I believe that global car technological development could reach matural stage, then it will infuence global car buyers number increases as well as this car technological mature development stage may also bring global rapid economic growth future non-manual driving car buyers and battery energy car buyers both number increases.

CHAPTER FIVE

Reengineering Management Science

What does reengineering management science mean? It is one kind of process reengineering is about innovating and changing , innovating the way work is done and changing the way people work together to get the task done. In fact, any organizations plan to survive, improvement is not an option. Hence, dramatic improvement is essential. However, I shall suggest " reengineering management skill" to help any organizations to achieve effective improvement, or raising efficiency or performance. But, process reengineering is difficult. To achieve effective reengineering managment skill, it must need time, creativity, even if the organization doe snot achieve effective reengineering management skill, if it ususally achieves more than 50% or more. Consequently, it can be achieved to effective reengineering managment skill absolutely. I shall explain whether how organization ought implement reengineering managment skill in order to achieve effective more than 50% level objective as below:

I assume that you are one organization CEO, a vice president,a trainer , a manager or a supervisor. You may attempt to implement process reengineering in action in order to design changes. However, each phase builds on the vision and research of the previous phase. If you desire dramatic improvement in one or more processes within your organization. You need to learn how to succeed plan for, design and implement a reengineered process. However, effective process reengineering may be your organization's chance to break ahead in an increasingly competitive business environment.

What is process reengineering ? It can be defined as the fundamental rethinking and redesigning of existing process tasks and operating structure to achieve dramatic improvement in process performance. What is the different between continuous process improvement and process reengineering. Although process reengineering needs to be spent cost and too time consuming. But, it can assist any organizations to lead to changing organizational structure lead to changing organizational structure and redesigning jobs to be better or to be improved.

Process reengineering is periodic and focuses on the achievement of dramatic improvement, redesigning how a process operates without being constrained by how things were previously long done. It aims to assist the traditional organization to add up to significant improvements, focuses on outcome and multiple gains. With process reengineering, process changes often go hand in hand with changes in job design, managment systems, training and retraining, organizational structure and information technology, e.g. improving frontline employees subprocess that is part of a higher-level process, with process reengineering, information systems technology often helps to improve in cycle-time reduction , informtation access, and avoiding paper waste for administration task.

Reengineering management skill may include these several aspects: Marketplace changes, e.g. your products or services is rapid changes, making incremental improvement, to existing processes, new product/ service development, geographic spread, if the process is typically " housed" within one or more physical locations (e.g. work groups / departments etc.) , multiple locations, particularly crossing countries and critical data exhange, customers / suppliers involvement (hand-on customer and supplier is desired with key customer and supplier of the process being reengineering, cost and staffing allocation is when to limited financial resources and periodic , part time involvement, part time reengineering efforts have commonly resulted in limited resources, increased frustration on the part of team members and missed expectations on the part of senior management for disadvantages, level of urgency is relatively low on the quality improvement.

Reengineering is more appropriate if an existing process is failing or when the suitation is drastic and significant improvement must be achieved in a relatively short period of time. Core elements of process reengineering may include: Purchases new hardware and software, redesigns jobs and train representatives when the way customer service representatives need often to handle customer complaints. For example, reengineering aims to help the representatives to attract a greater number of customers to become repeat customers and to raise the turnover of customer service to climb up within six months.

In general, the three phases for reenginerring management strategy include: Phase one: plan , determine " new process requirements, seek opportunities, analysis as is capability, envision desired state, indentify process performance gaps ; Phase two: Design, map the ideal process, complete preliminary work, set new goals and establish measures, create a new process flow chart. It aims to redefine process support requirements, develop change management plan. Final phase: Implement on the " trial run" basis, standardize the reengineered process, evaluate process performance on an ongoing basis.

How to select a process reengineering team? Should an interim team looks at the need for reengineering first? Should the team manage the process reengineering effort from beginning to end? Should team members be assigned to the team for the entire duration or just need? Should team members be selected for first-hand knowledge of the process being reengineering, authority level or for other reasons?

Determining new process requirements involves researching what your customers want and what the marketplace offers and determining what operating requirements you need set for the new process to meer demands. In the reginnering process, cost of labor is essential. The end result is that profitability decreases, because they had to hire additional help to spead up the time. Now if the goal was time, reduction because customers demanded it and profitability was not a factor, then the effort could be considered successful.

Consequently, when you feel that your organization needs to be implement any kinds of new reengineering management strategy , you must need to consider these issues, such as are there any parts of the process than can be eliminated ? Can technology help, what tools or equipment can improves the process? How will they improve it? Is new computer hardware or software necessary for your reengineering effort, will you need to provide training for any new equipment or to use already existing equipment? Where the delays in your current processes are, steps are designed in the correct order? Where you are getting the least account of return?

Organizational change and development reengineering strategy case

Giornl coffee company is a small collection of individuals with many ideas and a pressing need for financial capital. The founding partner, provided expertise in unscale speciality coffees and European style coffee bars and coffee houses. It hopes to raise capital. it decided to do little advertiseing, relying instead of seattle's established coffee culture to provide initial interest among potential customers. It also needs to handle the increasing customer traffic challenge. It decided to hire additional people and planned for expansion. Everyone did every thing. One staff needs to make sandwich meat at his desk in the business office, when another waited on customers, cleaned tables, and obtaned additional financial capital. Everyone worked long hours, but motivation was high. Owners , managers and baristas who made and served the various coffee drinks were in the venture together and were inspired by the possibility of fundamentally elevating the coffee experience in Seattle and beyond. It is one good reengineering strategy to change this coffee shop employee attitude to be positive emotion in order to satisfy coffee customer service and coffee taste provision need.

New technology reengineering strategy case

Polaroid corporation has become a classic case, showing the outcome of being too slow to change. It introduced instant photography to the market and at time was among the top 50 corporation in U.S. However, in 2001, it declared bankruptcy. Polaroid's problem was its failure to adapt in a timely way to technological change. It lost its market because it was too slow in recognizating the importance of digital imaging technology and then too slow in changing after competitors developed digital cameras.

The development of a new technology created the need for the change. Although the top managers are responsible for instituting such changes, managers and accociates lower in the organization must help because of their knowledge of the environment (markets, customers, competitors, technology, government regulations). All managers should actvely scan the environment for changes and help to identify external opportunities and threats. Unfortunately, managers did bot perceive the threat to their existing business quickly enough to transform the firm. After learning of the need for a change. These managers began the difficult process of designing and implementing a new approach, but they were able to do so in time to avoid failure. Competitors developed and introduced new cameras using digital technology before Polaroid could do and it lose a substantial share of its market. So this camera manufacturing firm can not achieve reengineering strategy before competition market increases. So it became loss.

In general, this camera firm encountered ought feel these pressures for its organizational reengineering change. They may include: aspiration performance discrepances, technology advances, introduction of removal of government regulations, changes in societal values, shifting political dynamics, changes in demogrpahics, growing international interdependence, life cycle forces. All of these factors may influences it can not achieve reengineering change strategy easily.

Life cycle forces

When any organizations feel need reengineering change. Organizations tend to encounter predictable life-cycle forces as they grow. Not every organization experiences the same forces in the same way as others, but most organizations face similar pressures. Although several models of the organizational life cycle have been proposed, an integrative model best highlights the key pressures that organizations experience. The model had four stages. Entrepreneurial , collectively , formalization and control, and elaboration.

In the entreprensurial stage, founders and perhaps a fre initial managers and associates develop ideas for products and services, acquire capital and take actions to enter a niche in the marketplace. This is an exciting time, but after the market is entered and success is achieved, growth requires founders to add managers and associates. Processes must be introduced for selecting , training and corrdinating these individuals.

In the collectivity stage, founders, managers and associates continue to emphasize product or service development and fund raising. Individuals in the young firm tend to feel like a family as they pursue the vision that attracted them to the firm. Individuals often work long hours for relatively low pay. As the firm continues to grow, formal process mus tbe incorporated to resolve or prevent coordination and control problems.

In the formalization and control stage, staffs are guided by formal processes and rules, a strict division of labour, and a stable organizational structure. And they emphasize efficiency more than innovation. Functional disciplines , such as accounting and operation managemenr are elevated in status. As the firm contiues to grow, more rules and procedures are often added, along with a greater number of management levels.

Finally, in the elaboration stage, managers and associates experience a more balances, mature organization. formal rules and processes exist empowered lower level managers and associate. Efficiency concerns with concerns for innovation and renewal. (reenginering changing strategy) is needed.

Why does reenginering strategy need to plan change?

How does an organization respond to pressure for change? On possibility is planned change, which involves deliberate efforts to move an organization or a subunit from its current state to a new state. Planned change may be evoluation, or can be more revolutionary, involving major changes in a shorter period of time. To effectively move the organization from one state to another. Those managing the change must consider a number of issues in three distinct parts of the change process.

Process of planned change is typically thought of as a three phase process that moves an organization from an undersirable stte through a difficult transition period to a desireable new state. Although, researchers tend to agree on the nature of these three phases, different names for the phases have been used by different people. However, the process of planned change may include these three stages:

Unfreezing stage: provide rational for change, create minor level of anxiety about not changing, create sense of psychological safety , concerning change.

Moving stage: provide information that supports proposed changes, bring about actual shifts in behavior.

Refreezing stage: implement new evaluation systems, create levels of anxiety about not changing, implement new hiring and promotion systems. However, style of change may include: urgency level, if the change is urgent, a participatory approach should not be used, as it tends to be time consuming. Degree of support, if the idea of changing is supported by a wide variety of people, a particpatory approach is less necesary as well as referent and expert power of change leaders, when change leaders are admired and are known to be knowledgeable about pertinent issues, a participatory approach is less necessary. So, reeengineer strategy must need to consider change style in order to achieve the right time change.

CHAPTER SIX

How Technology Influences Consumer Behavior To Bring Reduce Cost

Can technology influence human shopping behavioral change?

Nowadays, technological development has reached mature stage, whether technological mature stage may bring positive or negative shopping emotion influence to global consumers. I shall aplly internet inventin or ecommerce shopping channel tool to explain whether internet technology can bring postive or negative influence to global consumer behavior in behavioral economic view.

Internet is a good technological tool, it brings e-commerce business chance. In fact, commonly, global has have many businessmen choose to use internet channel to carry on their products transactions between global online-buyers and their electronic websites. So, global many shoppers had begun to feel online shopping is more convenient to compare visiting shops shopping. Their shopping behaviors have been changed from internet technological tool. Global has many shoppers choose to buy any products from any overseas or local businessmen their web stores. They only need to spend time to find any businessmen their webstores to choose the most suitable products to pay visa to buy from their webstores. at homes. So, in general, global had have may shoppers had changed their shopping behaviors from visiting shops to visiting webstores at homes often.

So, it seems that internet technological tool had influenced global many shops disappear, but internet webstores will be replaced their actual shops on streets. Some of businessmen either they choose webstores to replace shops or choose websotes and shops both or still keep shops only. Hence, internet tool influences global businessmen have three kinds of products sale channels to let globa local and overseas consumers to choose how to buy their products.

However, in fact, many of global shoppers, youngers and olders had begun to accept to buy any products from webstores. They feel to spend time to leave homes to visit shops , their shopping behaviors will be wasted time to not essential part to their daily lives. Hence, since internet technological invention, it had changed many consumers their traditional visiting shops shopping habit to change to buying products from webstores channel.

However, on the one hand, internet creates webstores ecommerce shopping channel to let global many consumers do not need to leave homes to go to shopping. It brings negative visiting shops shopping emotion to global general consumers nowadays. But on the other hand, it also brings positive visiting internet webstores shopping emotion to global general consumer nowadays. So, it seems that global many consumers feel that they often do not need to spend much time to go out shopping. Many global consumers feel convenient and enjoy to choose any products to buy from different internet webstores, when the online buyer chooses the most suitable product, he she only needs to pay visa card to buy the product from the online seller's webstore conveniently at home.

Hence, online shopping can bring economic benefit to online buyers, e.g. avoiding walking time or spending transport fare to visit the shop to go to shopping, shortening or reducing shopping time to do another important matter.

On conclusion, global many consumers began feel online shopping can bring more economic benefits on shortening shopping time, avoiding transport fare spending aspect. So, online shopping will be popular shopping behavior for future long time. It may encourage global many shoppers can make rapid shopping decision in short time in order to carry on any products buying transaction to global any one online shopper in short time easily in behavioral economic view. So, global many businessmen had begun to build themselves one attraction webstore in order to persuade different countries consumers to choose to click themselves webstores from internet channel to buy any kinds of products in short time easily.

So, internet technology had changed consumers traditional shopping behaviors to build positive online shopping emotion as well as raise online sellers' any products sale chance easily in behavioral economic view.

Why and how human behavior may influence the country's economic growth or recession?

When one country has many people choose to do the same matter for one period, whether their behavior may influence the country's pvera; economic growth or recession . I shall attempt to indicate cases toexplain their relationship as below:

For flowing rubblish behavioral case example, do you feel that when the country has many people often flow rubblish on the streets, instead of their flowing rubblish behavior may bring streets dirty? But, their flowing rubblish behavior may explain that this country has people may have enough money to buy food to ear, or enough cloths to wear, enough bottles of water to drink, even they may have enough money to buy new television, radio, refrigeraters , washing machines, desktops or laptops electronic home products from old to new to use in order to satisfy their living needs. So, when they flow old electronic home products, their flowing old home electronic products behaviors may seem that they have enough money to buy other new home electronic products to replace old home electronic products to use at homes.

However, it seems thaat this country ought have many people have jobs to do. So, many of them, they can easy to make purchase decison to flow any old home electronic products and buy any new home electronic products to use . Because this country has many people have jobs to do. So, they can often not use old home electonic products to become rubblishs to flow on streets after they had bought any kinds of new home electronic homes.

In fact, it also implies that this country's economy grows rapidly. So, many businesses can glow up rapdly. When they expanded their businesses, they must need to increase employees number in order to let they help themselves to raise productivity or serve their clients absolutely. So, when the country has many businesses can grow up, it seems that its economy must be better or it is improved to compare past. Due to many different kinds of home electronic products had been often bought to use by this country people in this period. So, this country's any streets can be observed that expensive electronic home products were flowed on streets anywhere. then, this country will have many electronic home products sellers can sell their home electronic products very easily. When this country has many people can find any kinds of jobs to do easily. So, due to unemploymen rate had been decreasing.

In behavioral economic view, as this many electronic home products rubblish country case, we can observe this country may have many people have jobs to do. So, consumption number has been increased long time. So, cheap food, or expensive home electronic products may be rubblish on any streets. This country's people , their flowing rubblish behaviors may be explained that many of people have enough jobs to do, so they have ability to buy any good taste food to eat or buy any kinds of expensive electronic home products to use. So, this country's economy may be improved for this long period. So, in behavioral economic view, when this country can have many electronic home products rubblishs are flowed on anywherer in streets frequently. It seems that this country will have many people have jobs to do, so it causes they often change old home electronic products or replaced them easily, when they have enough income to spend to buy any kinds of new home electronic products to use at homes easily. Moreover, their flowing old electronic home products behaviors also indicate that this country has many people their salaries may be increased in possible from their emplyers. When this country can have many different kinds of home electornic products are sold. It means that this country's electronic home products needs or demand had been increasing, due to many people have jobs to do and income increases to excite their living of needs also improve. Consequently, this country may seem have better economic improvement. We can observe from this country's electronic home products rubblish increasing income in theis period.

On conclusion, this country ought experience economic growth at this period. So, " flowing expensive electronic home rubblish increasing number " may seem that this country's economic growth is rapidly in this period, due to many people have jobs to do as well as salaries increase in this period.

Technology how impacts human behavior changing?
Technology how influences human behavior to bring changing? For example, online share purchase and sale transaction from smart phone brings share investor can do share buying or selling transation in any where and any time conveniently, non manual driving auto vehicle, bring car owner feels comfortable and spends free time to do other matter, e.g. reading, listening mucis in himself or herself car freely. electrical energy vehicle can help car owner to reduce air polluton and it can brings the drivers do not feel drive long time in any journeys in order to avoid air pollution for environmental protection responsible car drivers in our societies. Thus, they will drive long time in any journeys when they can

drive electronic energy cars to replace oil energy cars.

However, online technology can also bring consumers can choose to stay at homes to buy any things from seller individual online webstore conveniently. Such as online technology can bring shoppers do not need to spend much time to visit shops to buy any things. They can choose any kinds of products from any online sellers individual online webstores conveniently at homes. Online technology excite busy consumers can make purchase decision easily as well as it can help online sellers sell any kinds of products from internet easily.

In behavioral economic view, technology can change human behavior to be improved, it can let human feels comfortable, more free time ro use, rapid making any decisions, such as apply smart phones to make share purchase or sale transaction decision, online shopping decision, even travelling any where decision in short time, when the traveller finds the most cheap hotel accommodation room price and air ticket price frm any travel agent online tourism webstore, then the potential travel customer can follow the online hotel accommodation price and air ticket price data to make decision when to buy the air ticket from the airline travel agent or make decision when to prebook which hotel accommodation room to go to the country to travel from online travel agent tourism webstores. So, technology can encourage global any country travelers to make anywhere to trvel rapidly. If the traveler can find the country's general hotel rooms and airline tickets prices had been decreasing more sightly. The traveler may make travel decision to choose the country to travel in short time, then he/she can prebook the country;s any hotel room and airline ticket to pay by visa fraom the country's any hotel and airline travel agent webstores., before one week, even one month or more easily. Hence, online technology can also encourage traveler individual frequent travel times to be increased, due to global travelers can find any hotel rooms and airline tickets prices from internet conveniently at homes. They do not need to spend time to visit any airline travel agent to enquire travel choice country's hotel rooms prices and airline ticket prices. They can compare global travel of countries choices ' all hotels rooms and airline agents air tickets prices to make prebook airline seat and hotel room decision before one week, one month even six months early.

On conclusion, online technology can encourage global travelers can make travelling any where and when traveling time desicions easily. It can excite tourism industry develops in long time. Also, such as electricity cars invention can encourage environment protection car owners do car purchase decision easily, because they can choose to drive electronic energy cars to replace oil energy cars in order to avoid air pollution occurs easily. So, electronic cars can increase electronic car purchasrs number, due to many of environmental protection attitude of car owners can choose to drive electricity cars to bring air cleans, even non -manual driving cars can encourage lazy driving and free time driving car owners to choose to buy non-manual (artificial intelligent) cars to drive , because they can spend much free time to read, listen music or do any matters in themselves cars, they do not need to drive cars, robotic (AI) auto driving machine is such one non-manual driver to help them to drive themselves cars confidently. So, non-manual driving cars can attract lazy and enjoying free time driving car owners to choose to buy to replace traditional manual cars to drive easily. Moreover, online share transaction can help any share investors to make share buying and selling decision in short time easily. When they can apply smart phones technological tool to carry on share buying and selling activities easily. They can observe any share rising or falling price suitation from smart phones in any where any any time easily. So, smart phone technology can help global any shareholders to make share purchase and sale transaction easily. So, technology can encourage human makes decision in short time rapidly.

How and why employees behaviors may influence economy development?

In behavioral economy view,I believe the country's any organizational employees behavior may bring indirect relationship to influence the country's long term economic development. I shall indicate past manufacture industry social development period to explain their relationship. For many countries' past business activities had belonged to manufacturing industry, such as US, UK past before 1980 year, it focused on steel manufacturing and steel manufacturing related machine products. So, US, Uk developed countries manufacturing industries may be past main country's economic income sources. I assume US , UK past had one million number different kinds of industries. They ought had about seven houndred thousand number organizational businesses were belonged to manufactured industry. They may include:
Steel manufacturing and steel related machine manufacturing, e.g. vehicle manufacturing, home appliances, e.g. washing machine, television, radio, refrigerate cooler, heater, air condition etc. different kinds of different kinds

of steel -related manufacturing machine, they were manufactured from US, UK steel machine manufacturers. So, US, Uk the other three hundred thousand number industry may be general service industry, e.g. hotel service, restaurent, cinema, public transport service, tourism lesiure , wine bar, supermarket etc. different kinds of non-manufacturing industries business organizations were operated in UK, US past before 1980 year.

So, in UK, US developed countries industry development history, they ought have high percentage of businesses belonged to steel related manufacturing machine and steel products. Also, in the past before 1980 year, US, Uk business employers , they employed many workers are manufacturing workers. They needed to spend long time to work in factories. They were skillful workers, and they are trained to manufacturing cars, washing machine, television, heater, etc. even steel itself different kinds of steel related products to prepare to deliver to their shops to sell to US, Uk local or overseas clients.

So, I believe that past UK, US ought employ many employees, they belonged to skillful manufacturing workers, manufacture increasing steel machine or steel related machine number of products rapidly daily. So, if UK, US had had many of these manufacturing factories owned high skillful workers, then their manufacturing steel-related machine or steel both kinds of products number must be influenced to raise rapidly. Consequently, their steel machine manufacturing products would been exported to overseas or would been sold to local both markets , they may be influenced to raise sale number. They (these manufacturing workers) needed to be trained to know how to manufactur these different kinds of machine products in the efficient teams and they ought to be trained to raise their efficiencies in order to shorten time to manufacturing many kinds of steel related manufacturing machine or steel itself products rapidly. So , if their efficiencies and manufacturing performance was improved, these US, UK any one manufacturing worker and their teams ought achieve raising productivities significantly.

Hence, when past UK, US manufacturing industry development period, if these two countries' any manufacturing factories could have many manufacturing workers could be trained to be skillful and proficient manufacturing workers. Then, in past every day to these factories workers, they ought help their steel or steel related manufacturing employers to raise any kinds of machine or steel products number in every team. So, when past in the manufacturing industry development, US, UK could have many factories' manufacturing workers themselves steel or steel related machine products manufacturing skill could be trained to to improve to any kinds of these machine or steel manufacuring products quality as well as their products number could be influenced to raise by themselves skillful improvement significantly every day.

Then, what would be influenced to occur to past UK, US manufacturing industry period? In behavioral economic view, when these two manufacturing industry developed countries, such as UK, US , if they had many factories workers can be trained to improve their skill in order to achieve any kinds of steel or steel-related machine products quality could be improved as well as products manufacturing number could be also increased absolutely.

In consequence, past UK and US both countries ought increase themselves any kinds of steel and steel related machine products number to be supplied to themselves local shops to let local clients to choose any one kind of machine manufacturing products to buy easily as well as they could also export to supply overseas any countries to buy their different kinds of steel or steel related machine products to let overseas steel or steel related manufacturing machine product buyers, they can have many of these different kinds of these steel or steel-related different kinds of manufacturing machine from UK and UK these both countries easily to compare other countries.

On conclusion, I believe that past US, and UK macro manufacturing industry income GDP would increase significantly. So, they would have good economic growth performance because when many of these manufacturing workers themselves manufacturing effort could be improved. So, it explained when employees manufacturing abilities can influence economic growth indirectly.

Robots invention whether they can help organizations to raise efficiencies or inefficiencies?

In behavioral economic view, in any organizations, when the organization hopes its worker teams can raise efficiencies , the organization may choose to increase more workers number and/or it can provide training to improve these workets themselves skills in order to raise their efficiencies. For one warehouse example, when the warehouse increases many goods , they are needed to delivered these goods from the shelves to the delivering destination locations. If this warehouse supervisors feel these workers themselves goods delivery speeds are slow, which is possible due to this warehouse's workers number is not enough. So, this warehouse supervisor ought increase workers number in order to increase their goods delivery speed in order to deliver goods from the shelves to every indicated goods delivery destination in order to let any one lorry driver can transport the right kinds of goods and ensure the accurate goods number to transport to any one client home rapidly.

However, if this warehouse supervisor planed to buy several warehouse goods delivery robots to assist these warehouse workers to find the right kinds of goods from shelves and then deliver to the right destination location in the warehouse. So, these warehouse orkers can concentrate on counting the accurate goods number and ensuring the right kinds of goods in order to prepare to let lorry drivers to transport these goods to these goods of buyers themselvers homes rapidly. Consequently, in the first step, robots can concentrate on finding th right goods from shelves and delivers them to the right goods transportation of location destination. Then, in the second step, these warehouse workers can concentrate on counting the accurate goods number and ensuring the right kinds of goods in order to prepare to put them to the lorry. Consequently, when warehouse robots and warehouse workers can cooperate to work together, the most important, robots, can deal on finding the right kinds of goods and deal on delivering the accurate number of goods of job duty as well as these warehouse workers can only concentrte on counting the right kinds of goods number in order to avoid it has none any mistake of wrong kinds of goods and inaccurate goods of delivery number to be transported to the lorry and to deliver to any one buyer's home.

So, it seems that warehouse robots ought help any one warehouse worker to raise himself efficiency and avoid goods delivery of mistake occurrence easily as well as their help to warehouse workers that can let any one goods buyer feels their goods can be delivered to their homes rapidly. Moreover, warehouse robots can also help these warehouse workers to raise efficiencies because warehouse robots can help them to shorten goods delivery time between any one shelf and any one goods delivery destination of location in the warehuse because robots may help them to find the right kinds of goods from the right shelf in the short time. So, any one worker does not need to spend long time to seek anywhere is the right shelf location for the kind of goods when the kind of goods are needed to deliver to the buyer's home from lorry. Warehouse robots can help them to do this aspect of " finding the goods from the right shelf in short time job duty". So, any one warehouse worker only needed tospend less time to do the counting of any right kind of goods number and ensuring the right kind of goods job duty. Consequently, this warehouse 's any one worker, his any one kind of goods delivery time may be reduced, because robots' assistance and they may have more confidence to avoid mistake to deliver the wrong number of goods and/or the wrong kind of goods to any one goods buyer's home.

On conclusion, it seems that warehouse robots ought may help any one warehouse worker to raise efficiency for any one team in the warehouse as well as the warehouse any one supervisor does not need to spend much time to observe any one worker individual performance for " goods delivery job duty aspect" because their goods delivery job duty that had been replaced to do by these several warehouse robots. Robots can achieve the more accurate of right kinds of goods and the right number of goods delviery job performance to compare any one of human warehouse worker themselves right kinds of goods of delivery and right number of goods of delivery job performance. So, when robots can participate to cooperate with this warehouse's any one worker to do their goods of delivery job duty in this warehouse every day. Then, robots can raies any one of supervisor individual confidence in order to let they do not need to spend time to observe any one of worker individual whose goods of delivery job performane. They can concentrate on supervising any one worker whose goods transport to lorry in the final step in order to avoid to deliver wrong goods number and / or wrong kind of goods to any one goods buyer's home every day. Consequently, this warehouse's overall teams of their delviery of goods performance many be improved by robotss' participatin to goods of delivery task as well as this warehouse's oveall teams themselves efficiencies may be influenced to raise by robots' goods of delivery task participation.

Why social behavior may influence organizational strategy needs to be changed ?

Why any organizations need to know whether nowadays social behaivor how has been changing in order to implement the kind of the most right strategy to achieve the profit aim pursue in possible. I shall indicate nowadays ecommerce or online, customer shopping behavior to explain above question concerns they ought have close relationship between social behavior and organizational strategic choice or organizational behavioral changing need.

On nowadays ecommerce business, or online shopping model, this kind of shopping model in global many young and old age consumers like to apply internet tool to choose any country sellers website stores in order to stay at home to buy any kinds of products from themselves webstores in global societies.

In fact, online shopping model had been popular for long time above to twenty years. Most of global sellers will make decision to design themselves webstores in order to attract global many online buyers to choose to buy their products from themselves webstores. So, it seems that social consumers purchase behaviors had been changed to online shopping from internet invention.

Hence, social consumers purchase behavioral changes may influence any organizations' strategies need to be changed from visiting shops purchase strategy model to online purchase strategy model, if the seller still concentrate on concentrate on considerate how to design itelf , but neglects to considerate how to design itself webstore, e.g. how to design attract product photos to put on itself webstore, how to arrange sale price information location to be putted on webstore and visa card payment location on itself webstore in order to let any one online buyer can feel very easier to buy itself any kinds of products from itself webstore. Then, its potential online buyers will be influenced to increase number when they can find this online seller itself any kinds of products photes and every kinds of product sale price information and visa card payment channel locations easily from itself webstore.

So, it implies that nowadays any one seller ought need to design one webstore to let any one online overseas and domestic consumers can have chance to click itself webstore to choose any one kind of product to buy conveniently when he/she does not hope to leave him/her home to go to shop, because nowadays social shopping behaviors had been influenced to change when internet invention, them it gives another online purchase method to replace visiting shops purchase method to global any one buyer in nowadays societies.

So, if nowadays any one seller still concentrate on how to design itself shop display in order to put any kinds of product on shelf in order to let any one visiting shop customer to find the kind of product to buy, but it neglects to change to choose to pursue another new technological shopping method, such as webstore purchase method in order to implement effective strategy to design the most right webstore as well as in order to attract global overseas and local consumers to find itself webstore easily from website and find its any one kind of product phots and sale price and visa card payment button in order to choose to buy itself any kinds of products in the short time. Consequently I believe that the seller will lose many customers from overseas and local when its other same or similar product sellers choose to design themselves webstores in order to let global any one product buyer can buy themselves any one kind of product when they can pay visa card to buy their products from them webstores conveniently when they stay at home habitly. Then, the seller will lose many global potential customers in long time.

On conclusion, in behavioral economic view, any consumer behavioral social changing, which will influence any in order to avoid customers number loses significantly . In future time, organizations need to make rapid decision in order to implement the most reasonable and the most useful strategy in order to avoid global potential customers number reduces or lose them in long time. So, social behavioral changing environment ought influence any global organizations need to decide how to change themselves strategies in order to avoid customers loses significantly in future time.

How and why human behavior may influence economic growth or recession?

May ourselves daily behaviors influence our global societial continue economic growth or recession? Do they have cause and effect close relationship between human behaviors and global economic growth or recession? I shall apply behavioral economic theory to analyze and explain whether ourselves daily behaviors and our global societial economic growth or recession which have close cause and effect relationship as below:

Every country itself economic development must depend on any business activities, otherwise, any kinds of business activities must need ourselves business activities or behaviors in order to achieve any business activities as well as achieve the country's overall economic development in macro view. However, any country's overall business activites or behaviors which must depend on any kinds of individual businessmen, themselves employees daily working behavior or activity or performance in order to help them to attract or increase many clients number to acieve " earning profit" aim. So, it seems that any individual business, itself overall every department individual working behavior is one main factor to influence the company's overall business performance.

For agricultural fruit and meat food farming industry example, such as New Zealand is a farming main target industry country. It had had many New Zealanders were daily themselves own farming businesses for many years. Their farming businesses include growing fruit, sheep, cow, pig pork, meat etc. food sale business. If the New Zealand farmer owned a large size farming land, then he will choose either growing fruit or feeding sheeps, pigs, cows to be meat to to transport to New Zealand supermarkets to help them to sell to their farmers meet to New Zealanders in order to earn profit. Thus, if the New Zealand farmer owned large size of farming lands, then he needs to employ many farming employees (farming workers) to help him to carry on farming business daily tasks, e.g. picking up friuts, feeding pigs, cows, sheeps to eat food daily. These daily farming jobs are very important to influence this New Zealand farmer's meats or fruits sale number whether they can be easy or diffcult to sell in New Zealand supermarkets , if these farming workers can own encough farming knowledge or skill to know how to pick up fruits method and make judgement to know whether it is right time to pick up the kind of fruits from the trees , as well as know how feed this pigs, sheeps, cows to eat food in order to let they are better health. Consequently, their farming behaviors which can let these animals can provide the best taste and enough meat from these animals to let New Zealander to buy to eat from New Zealand any one supermarket. Even these New Zealand farming workers can know whether the kinds of fruits, e.g. oranges, apples, gapes etc. fruits whether they ought be picked up from the trees at the right time. Consequently, they can make judgement to decide to pick up any kinds of the best taste fruits to let any one New Zealander to buy to eat from any one supermarket in New Zealand. Otherwise, if they do not make judegement to know whether the kind of fruit ought not be picked up because they still need longer time to continue grow up to increase fruit size and better taste from the trees in order to let any one fruit buyer can feel better taste when they eat this kind of fruit later. If they can buy this kind of fruit to eat later, then this New Zealand farmer's his fruit buyers can buy the best taste of this kind of fruit to eat from an yone supermarket in New Zealand. Consequently, many New Zealand supermarkets will choose to buy any kinds of fruits from this farmer fruit supplier when they feel this farmer's fruits can provide more better taste fruits to compare other farmers' fruits.

Thus, due to New Zealand is one farming main income source country. It's any kinds of fruits and meats need to be export to overseas to sell , instead of local sale. It's GDP percent is very high to whole country 's overall income source. So, any one New Zealand farmer individual and any one farming worker individual working behavior will influence its economy whether it is influenced to grow or recession possible. Moreover, it also seems that farming workers' farming knowledge and skill will influence themselves farming daily activities to achieve the aim of the number of increase or decrease to any kinds of fruits whether they are better taste or the number of increase of decrease to any kinds of meats whether they are better taste to supply to any one New Zealand fruit or meat buyers to eat from any one New Zealand supermarket. So, it implies that any one New Zealand farming worker individual farming behavior may influence any kinds of fruits or any kinds of meat taste because they are transported to any one supermarket to sell in New Zealand.

Consequently, if New Zealans had many farmers can teach god farming knowledge and skill to let their any one farming workers know how to decide judgement to decide when it is right time to pick up any kinds of fruits from trees , or how to grow them on soil in order to let they can grow rapidly. Then, many different kinds of fruits can be provided to let any one New Zealanders can eat the best taste of fruits when their fruits are supplied to any one New Zealand supermarkets. Even, if they knew how to feed foods to pigs, cows, sheeps to eat daily. Then they can be more health and they can provide the best taste of meats to let any one New Zealanders can buy their meats from any one New Zealand supermarkets. Moreover, their fruits and meats can be transported to overseas to let any one country fruits or meats buyers can choose any kinds of New Zealand meats and fruits to buy to eat from themselves countries supermarkets. Then, many overseas fruit and meat buyers will perfer to choose New Zealand any kinds of fruits or meats to buy to compare other countries fruits or meats to buy when they go to any one local supermarkets.

On conclusion, it seems that New Zealand farming workers themselves farming behavior may influence their farming employers any kinds of fruits or meats sale number and income because their farming task behaviors must influence whether their fruits or meats taste are the better taste or worse taste to compare their other local farmers (the farmer competitors) whose fruits or meats taste. If tthe farmer's any one farming worker can be trained to learn how to know to feed animals skill and when is the most right time to pick up any kinds of fruits from trees or how to grow them on the soil methods. Due to these farming worker individual farming behavior may influence his different finds of fruits and meats sale number to be increase or decrease, so these any one New Zealand farmer must need to depend on any one farming worker whose farming working methods, if their farming working behaviors can be the best to influence any kinds of fruits to grow rapid or any kinds of pigs, cows, sheeps animals grow up rapidly , then their sale number may be increase significantly and their taste can be improved to let any New Zealand or overseas meat or fruit buyer to buy to eat to feel from any one New Zealand or overseas supermarkets, then New Zealand's agriculture industry must be influenced to increase. In the world, any one fruit or meat buyer must choose to buy New Zealand's fruit and meat to eat in prefer to compare other countries' fruits and meats. So, New Zealand's GDP may be influenced to raise from any one New Zealand farming worker individual farming working behaviors. It seems that New Zealand farmer fruit and meat sale number is depended on their eatting consumers demand more than their meat and fruit supply because if these NZ farmers can apply high technology method to grow good taste fruit or feed good taste meat to let global eatting customers to feel, their demand will increase, then NZ farmers will need to increase good taste fruit and good taste meat supply number to satisfy global meat and fruit eatting customer taste need.

CHAPTER SEVEN

Outsource saving cost strategy

Information Technology Outsourcing

In any organization information technology department, information system operations remain the predominant function outsourced, other functions are also being performed by external service providers and the relationship is between outsourcing and certain demographics: size, industry is formation intensity. The results suggest that system operations remain being performed by external service providers. Further, industry and information intensity has some influence on the extent of outsourcing of certain functions.

The first reason is cost reduction, trying to remain competitive and up-to-date is becoming a financial burden to many organizations. This is true particularly in fields, such as banking and financial services, health care and manufacturing. Hiring outsiders to handle part or even all of its information system often helps an organization to provide better services and maintain a competitive advantage. The information technology industry choice of outsourcing factor is related to size, industry type and information technology.

The second reason is technological and/or human resources in the management of the information technology infrastructure skill improvement. The information technology department outsourcing service to external service provider, includes the degree of internalization of technological resources and the degree of internalization of human resources. Some economists defined internalization of outsourcing service is as ownership is by the focal organization which takes on full control with profit and loss responsibility. Also who define outsourcing is as involving a significant use of resources, either technological and/or human resources, external to the organizational hierarchy in the management of the information technology infrastructure. So the information technology external service providers includes: applications development and maintenance, systems operations, networks/telecommunications management and user computing support, system planning and management purchase of application software, but excludes business consulting services, after-sale vendor services and the lease of telephone lines etc. outsourcing services.

The third reason is economics of scale in areas of hardware, software. This pressure is seen as the most significant factor driving today's corporate interest. An outsourcing service provision might be in a position to exploit economics of scale in areas of hardware, software and staff since it pools different kind of technological projects from many service receivers. Outsourcing information technological service can reduce the corporate's cost with the high level of IT investment, there are increasing pressures to move away from fixed expenditure, corporate overhead towards a more direct variable cost approach to control the IT operations. The IT costs can become predictable for overruns is often placed on the service provider. Outsourcing service can allow the service to gain immediate access to competitiveness in delivering products or services as well as to avoid of obsolescence risk, due to the changes in the nature of the IT infrastructure, the risk of obsolescence is high. Outsourcing can allow the service provider has the ability to diversify these risks across a broad range of service receivers. However, long term contracts might in spread the risk, the weakness is back to the receiver.

It seems outsourcing IT service has also these disadvantages: such as, loss of flexibility or managerial control. Outsourcing reduces real or perceived control over both quality real or perceived control over both the quality of software and the timetable of project since the work is now being carried out by people not under direct supervision. It also threats to long term career prospects to information system professionals because many of them do not find suitable. Is jobs or promising career paths in both areas of the corporation. Outsourcing also increases coordination cost. It may requires increasing time to communicate and coordinate with the service provider. Traditionally, the formal meeting cost of negotiating and monitoring the outsourcing contract are potentially wide ranging, indirect and substantial increasing, such as, additional releasing or transferring employees, in license transfer by software vendors and in re-negotiating contracts costs. So, the IT industry of profit motivates service provider might not be in the least interests of the outsourcing service receivers. Some IT service providers are in the business of maximizing their profit at any cost, this could run counter to a service receiver's interest.

●

Outsourcing or insourcing in human resource supply chain factor

To choosing of outsourcing or insourcing in human resource supply chain factor of the controlling service demanders needs to concern this issues: Should human resource activities be provided in house or should all or past of those activities be outsourced? The relationship between organizational structure and the HR function is an important variable. The individual activities that comprise HR systems include not only the employee life cycle from recruiting to termination, but also planning for organizational staffing needs and improving organizational effectiveness. How organizations need to outsource HR function to not care employees knowledge and skill is a factor to influence any organizations choose to outsourcing non core employees when which have no any right employees to be promoted to do the position. For example, firms engage in HR outsourcing to reduce management access HR expertise, achieve workforce flexibility, focus managerial resources and keep up with changing workplace negotiations. Also, supporting the tend is the availability of common technology platform, which can reduce costs for organizations and risks. However, organizations are afraid of losing some control over delivery of outsourcing services and finding themselves dependent on the vendor or liable for the vendors actions where there are both benefits and challenges may be informed by the structure of the relationship between client firms and these organizations offering the outsourced activities to client firms.

What variables are impacted by HR outsourcing of staffing? Which include: administrative costs for labor expense, client firm to HR relations, HR regulatory competency requirement, knowledge of cost factors, e.g. billing and pay rates, vendor markups and margins, vendor management competency requirement, client and vendor relationship, communication is between client managers and staffing vendor, employee data-available, data quality control, data security, match with job requirement, employee quality, inter-vendor competition, mining of client talent by vendor , quality content for preferred staffing vendor, standardization of business process (intra-company), strategic focus of client firm, demands on client managers vendor competency and external economic environmental viability.

However, it has dynamic relationship between the client firms and staffing vendors. Moreover, the models of human resource supply chain, every has different set of advantages and disadvantages for the client firms. The models can be relate to the decision making process on outsourcing of human resources. As strategic services tactic decisions have an important impact or selecting the particular HR outsourcing model that a client firm adopter. The another model is the balance of power and control over managing the control workers differ to decide what every worker individual skills or abilities outsourcing demand. Moreover, local contracting is also the predominant traditional model for outsourcing staffing with non-core employees. A client firm usually uses several staffing vendors to meet temporary staffing needs for seasonal functions, employee absences and special projects. The advantages of local contracting are high touch and high quality of service by staffing vendors, minimal bureaucracy, empowerment of hiring any high qualified employees to get the job done, and a relatively better fit between specific staffing vendors and functional needs.

The disadvantages of local contracting can increase costs from non-standardization of hiring practices and procedures across the client form, a significant amount of word of mouth and subjective quality issues, high local costs and client firm us subjected to the capabilities of the staffing vendors and contract employees. However, local HR contracting is the most flexible, high quality, but expense, inefficient and ineffective HR outsourcing model for the client firm. Another model is the working period to be decided to outsource HR contracting. In this situation, in the short term and on a day-to-day basis, the client firm aims to achieve on economy of scale with its staffing vendors. The total costs of temporary workers as well as internal costs for contracting with several different vendors are higher than if it needs one staffing vendors to meet all its needs. So, the client company can set the reasonable pricing that it pays for its temporary outsourcing staffs. Each staffing vendor secures a different rate range with each vendor as opposed as one contact. In the long term, it is benefiting, each specialized staffing vendor is able to fully work with each function needs temporary utilization is better than the average. Mismatches are fewer. Functional departments are able to receive a high quality / high touch service in any time period. Another model is the centralizing is when the department standardizes the staffing process to drive costs down of temporary workers. This tends to occur when a percentage of non-core employees reach a certain ratio of core employees. The advantages include more uniform standards in hiring process, billing rates and pay rates, departmental hiring managers can refocus their effort to choose outsourcing staffing, criteria may be established for a performed suppliers list and greater security for the staffing established vendors that offer higher quality services. The disadvantages include new departmental responsibilities in HR which decreases outsourcing efficiencies for the organizations daily administrative direction is rather than long term strategic direction. Usually lacking qualifications to fulfill the responsibilities, overall, centralizing of HR outsourcing is that firms can achieve more standardization which additional bureaucratic costs and the necessary non-core jobs do not get done as a need. Another model is purchasing HR, which manages staffing vendors from HR to the purchasing unit of an organizations. The goal is to continue cost reductions by increasing efficiencies. In conclusion, the main benefits of HR outsourcing include maintaining organizational control over the hiring process, application of purchasing capabilities for greater standardization in hiring processes pay rates and bill rates. So, any outsoucred HR organizations may be reduce hiring process cost.

●

Global outsourcing source strategy
in a value supply chain

What is global outsourcing source strategy in a departmental role? In a highly competitive global environment, many manufacturers are responded by setting and outsourcing relations for components and finished products with lower cost producers on a contractual electronic commerce department, (original equipment manufacturer basis). Outsourcing strategy is part of the value supply chain of corporate activated. Nowadays, global outsourcing increases organizational and technological capacity of firms and cooperating a network of remotely located external suppliers performing. These understanding the important roles that product designers, engineers and production managers and purchasing manager etc. play in global sourcing strategy empowerment. Specially, electronic commerce is popular to supply chain. For example, Toyota car manufacturing company, owns unique capabilities by designing and manufacturing certain car components in-house , i.e. insourcing. Toyota also outsource manufacturing activities, Toyota adopts purchasing necessary, but no strategic inputs from independent component suppliers on obtaining a lower cost for these inputs. For example, products would be belts, tires and batteries to vehicle products that are not customized and do not differentiate its products from its competitors. Toyota's outsourcing strategy is car strategic inputs provide differentiation, e.g. engine, transmission etc. are sources from suppliers based on strategic partnership to gain to access to suppliers' capabilities and it is also a conceptualize global outsourcing sourcing strategy to Toyota car manufacturing company.

How value chain outsourcing affects firm level performance. Global outsourcing strategy means to identify which production units that will serve which particular markets and how components will be supplied for production and thus included a number of basic choices, companies can make in decision how to serve various markets. Either choice relates to the use of inputs, assembly or production within the country to serve a foreign market or decides to use of internal or external supplies of components or finished products. In this outsourcing source input situation, the term sourcing is needed to describe how multi-national companies mange in of components and finished products in serving foreign and domestic markets. Sourcing decision making is both contractual point of view, the sourcing of major components and products are occurred by multi-national companies. First is from parents or their foreign subsidiaries. Second is from independent suppliers on a contractual basis. The first type of sourcing is known as insourcing. Otherwise, the second type of sourcing is referred to outsourcing. How to achieve economies of scale by outsourcing or insourcing sourcing input strategy? Therefore, the two outsourcing strategies are multi-faceted and require careful examination.

●

Outsourcing benefits in economic view

The two economists (Abrahamson & Rosenkopf, 1993) indicated that In long term, outsourcing can help to reduce fixed investment in finance view point, in-house manufacturing facilities and thus lower the breakeven point, which subsequently helps boost an outsourcing company whose return on equity (ROE). Thus, if any one corporate performance is evaluated on the basis of its contribution to the company's ROE. Also, in the short term or long term on resource inputs outsourcing view, early adopters of outsourcing strategy indeed experienced efficiency gains as they were able to reduce fixed investment in in-house manufacturing facilities and lows their ROE. But, later adopters may have different to gain institutions legitimacy or because of competition pressures in the industry, despite some inherent uncertainties about the long term costs and benefits of outsourcing strategy. It seems that outsourcing strategy was devised as any organization's policy makers to access trade linkages of benefits for short term or long term. Outsourcing strategy is a systematic analysis of the economic, political and regulatory implications indicates potential benefits along with a number of potentially negative side effects to any organizations. Then, outsourcing strategy will be caused this question: How to assess the risks and benefits of outsourcing for organizational sectors and nations both? The decision to change outsourcing behavior to carry a business activity may have profound implications for outsourcer and outsource receiver both, but little impact of the sector level. The common occurrence of industry decisions to outsource most manufacturing, including sale of factories, it created a new sub-sector, contract manufacturing. Otherwise, at a national level and public sectors become less distinct to outsourcing strategy. Public policy on outsourcing has stimulated extensive debate, privatization social justice and value for money etc. challenges.

●

What motivate outsourcing what is being outsourced risk and concerns?

Whether what motivate outsourcing, evidence of what is being outsourced risk and concerns? Outsourcing activities include: outsources manufacturing components and other value adding activities. Some focused on employment is outsourced another firm's employees carrying out tasks previously performed one's own employees. Outsourcing is an activity outside the organization's chosen core competencies. It seems outsourcing is a sub-contracting relationships between firms, all foreign production, hiring of workers in non-traditional jobs, such as control workers and temporary and part time workers.

What are the motivations for outsourcing reasons? Why outsourcing is needed to any organization. For example, it can enable firms to focus on core activities. The concept of focus originates in operation on a small, manageable, number of tasks at which the operation becomes excellent to specific technologies and as a risk of vertical integration advantages. Other benefits of outsourcing appear is literature on strategic management, operations management, purchasing and supply and innovations. Moreover, outsourcing can improve flexibility to meet changing business conditions, demands for products, services and technologies by creating smaller and more flexible clear evidence includes improved creditability image, greater workforce flexibility and avoiding being backed into specific assets and technologies are harder to measure. How outsourcing can improve company performance. For airline manufacturing industry example, Hill & Jones (1995) showed that the manufacture of a large portion of the Boeing 767 is Boeing's third largest commercial aircraft, which is outsourced to Japanese manufacturers, which include Fuji, Kawasaki and Mitsubish. As a result, only 10% of the value of the 767 Boeing is produced in-house. So, outsourcing is an attempt to enhance manufacturing air place industry competitiveness.

●

How can choose smarter outsourcing?

How can choose smarter outsourcing? Organizations hope to do sight options to save money, among themselves staff layoffs and a reduction of overhead costs, such as office space. Private companies have long outsourced in order to save time and money. During periods of economic growth, many organizations began to use outsourcing more frequently and staff workloads grew in proportion to increase budgets. Tasks such as conducting needs assessments, reviewing proposals, conducting site visits, monitoring and creating evaluations systems were increasingly given to outside contractors, consulting firms and independent consultants in the belief that external specialists could do the work more efficiently and effectively than company itself.

Nowadays, there is a growing stream of organizations need to research into the outsourcing of innovation activities within the innovation, management, marketing and economics disciplines. These organizations need to understand how with the outsourcing practice becoming more commonplace in their industry. However, their behaviors bring these two questions: Whether outsource or internalize innovation activities and the performance implications of this decision can support for both transaction cost and resource based arguments is examined with both theory bases showing substantial attention? Whether outsourcing innovation activities can lead to faster product development and cost savings? On advantages hand, it is possible that outsourcing may lead to higher costs and slower new product development. Further the technological uncertainty may have conflicting impacts on the outsourcing decision that are not yet well understand. When outsourcing product development has reduced costs and has proved speed to market. On disadvantages hand, outsourcing has also reduce product development time delays and higher quality concerns. Why to cause performance implications of outsourced innovation activities in transaction in cost economics and the resource-based view point? When outsourcing product development has been to reduce costs and has improved speed to market, outsourcing product development is not unlike other make or buy decisions. So, make vs buy decision is similar to logistic and IT outsourcing. Internalization of product development will be preferred when transaction costs are excessive. Otherwise, the market i.e. outsourcing will be selected when transaction costs are low. Transaction costs can include adaption, safeguarding and measurement costs. Adaption costs represent efforts to adjust contract to change conditions and are a result of environmental uncertainty. When a firm may have to revise on agreement with a partner company, this facing substantial penalties, due to an unstable market environments, the firm is likely to perform this function internally. Safeguarding costs characterize the costs of an outsourcing provider acting opportunities after investments have been made in the inter-firm relationship and are the result of transaction specific investment. Measurement costs include all expenses with confirming that contracts have been fulfilled passably. The contracting firm may face substantial costs to estimate quality for contractual services. When the sum total of these transaction costs is substantial, internalization will be favored.

●

What is environmental uncertainty factor?

Environmental uncertainty refers to unanticipated changes in circumstances surrounding an exchange in market uncertain and technological uncertainty. Market uncertainty is the fluctuation and unpredictability of demand. With respect to innovation projects, market uncertainty may cause frequent changes to the development, complications and adding expense to external contracting. These changes may necessitate renegotiation or cancellation of innovation contracts, which will likely carry prohibitive penalties (a term) transaction costs. These transaction costs promote internalization under high levels of market uncertainty. Otherwise, technological uncertainty environments, selecting market governance allows firms the flexibility to end relationship should technical requirements shift. It seems that market and technological external change factor will influence to benefits to any organizations to choose outsourcing strategy. On the other side, outsourcing can bring this question: Whether the offshore outsourcing of information technology jobs choice is suitable to any IT organizations? Nowadays. The offshore outsourcing if IT jobs from the United States has been enabled by a powerful influence of global economic demographic and technological forces. In fact, many IT companies were drawn to offshoring outsourcing because of the need for programmers to fix the Y2K problem in the late 1990- year. It is shortages of US programmers. Other factors driving this phenomenon include the wage gap between the US and developing countries, e.g. China and India, advances in technology, labor availability, expanding foreign markets and foreign government incentives. The spread of the offshoring phenomenon from low skill manufacturing to high wage white collar service industry jobs reduces the country's IT jobs critics, it represents the mobility for many US workers who saw post-secondary education as the route to a higher standard of living. The offshoring outsourcing of manufacturing and service jobs from the US to lower cost foreign nations become a national issue in a very short time. The impact of offshore outsource on the information technology sector gives outsourcing potential loss of millions of jobs at all wage levels and the critical contribution is the IT sector to US productivity growth. However, decisions about the locations of manufacturing or service facilities reflect market forces key factors include the size of local markets, capital availability and costs, labor availability skill levels and cost, logistic issues, reliability and infrastructure and IT in particular relationships with research institutions. All these factors will influence the choice of offshore outsource IT jobs strategy top any organizations.

●

Whether outsourcing will bring
what kind of work skills.

Whether outsourcing will bring what kind of work skills. Many employers choose outsourcing to employ employees. This core of our work is identifying trends which will transform global society and the global marketplace. How it influences our nature of work form health care to technology, the work place and human identity. A decade ago, workers worried about jobs being outsourced overseas. Today companies, such as Odesk and Liveops can assemble teams " in the cloud" to dosales, customer support and many other tasks. It seems outsoucring can influence many high technological job of changes. Global connectivity, smart machines and new media are just some of the drivers reshaping how we thank about work, what constitutes work and the skills, we shall need to be productive contributors in the future. As computer technology in the cloud will be used popularly to society. A signal is typically a small or local innovation that has the potenial to grow in scale and geographic distribution. A signal can be a new product, a new practice, a new market strategy, a new policy or new technology, such as online cloud computing files storage service method. It is an innovative social science method to computer users. However, this new computer files storage method influences outsourcing service of needs increasing. It will have key drivers and skills areas that will be most relevant to the technological workforce of the future.

It is estimates that by 2025 year, the number of Americans over 60 age will increase by 70%. The challenge of an aging population will come. What it means to age, individuals will need to rearrange their approach to their career, family life and education to accommodate their life plan. Increasing, people will work long past 65 age in order to have adequate resources for retirement. Multiple careers will be commmplace and lifelong learning to prepare for occupational change will see major growth. To take advantage of this well experienced organizations will have to rethink the traditional career paths in organizations, creating more diversity and flexibility. As the high technological cloud computing storage method is invented. Any organizations can save their files to the central cloud computer storage system website to save or find their files from website more easily. It will reduce their computer department expenditure and staff salary. So, outsourcing computer file storage service demands will be influenced to increase to any organizations as well as organizations will reorganize their computer department job nature to shape the kinds of social, economic and political organizations which inhabit. Outsourcing is a good solve method to assist organizations to pay cheap salary to employ many retired high age workers by contract or temporary or part time method to reduce their computer department's number of employees and the retired labors only need to pay cheap salary to learn how to use internet to help whose employers to save their files to their outsourcing computer storage service provider's central computer storage system every day efficiently. So, organizations do not need to employ many computer department staffs to avoid to pay much salaries to this computer department expenditure. They can choose outsourcing to pay cheap salaries to employ many retirement labors to assist them to do simple office storage job from internet channel efficiently and effectively. Hence, internet high technological innovation can influence office outsoucing of job duties increasing.

Whether domestic outsoucing in the America, what assesses trends and effects on job quality. Nowadays, US firms' use of contractors and independent contractors and its effect on job quality and inequality. Why firms choose contract out for certain functions and assess their predictions about likely impacts on job quality, stagnant wages, growing inquality and the deterioration of job quality are among the most important challenges facing the US economy today. Although any country's domestic outsourcing , firms' use of contractors, franchises and independent contractors any one of these factors is a potentially important influence to companies reduce compensation and shift economy risk to workers. However, the domestic outsoucing takes place on a much larger scale and effects many more workers than has been recognized ranging from low wage service workers, security guards, warehouse workers and hotel housekeepers to professionals and technical workers, such as programmers, health care technicians and accountants. These tends are part of structural change in the organization of production to influence quality of jobs and the nature of employment contract after outsourcing jobs are popular. The quality of jobs include wages, benefits, employee skills and training and mobility opportunities and job security as well as inequality across jobs. Domestic outsoucing concerns these issues: such as employment and labor law, the provision of health, pension and other workplace benefits. However, any companies choose outsourcing of employment reasons include, such as that it relates how management choices to pursue value added or cost focused strategies. Contracting out is difficult to define because a large part ot economic activity has always occurred through business-to-business transactions, as captured in macro-economic input-output models. Outsoucing job employment method can influence any one labor's individual quality of jobs. Usually, international companies choose the offshoring of work in global supply chains. Until recently, the domestic counterpart outsourcing employment method has grown supply chains to domestic or regional outsoucing employment.

What factors cause domestic outsourcing and whether firm decisions about what to retain in-house and what to outsource have changes over time. Some evidence suggests that firms have responded by focusing on their core competencies and outsourcing low value added tasks as well as higher value added specialized functions. Advanced technologies have facilitated this process by allowing firms to outsource entire functions ans more easily monitor contractors as well as employees who work, leading to new forms of networked production and rise of specialized outsouring employment firms. Domestic outsoucing influences the changes of job quality, benefits, hours, workload, job stability, schedule stability and occupational safety, health, incidence of wage theft and access to training and promotions. Predictions are less clear for job requiring professional or technicial or specialized skills or those that are outsourced to large and diversified outsourced contractors. Types of outsourced contracts include: suppliers or vendors of products, such as manufacturing inputs or services, such as business services or staffs service or staffing firms, franchisees and independent contract, such as freelancers, independent contracts or non demand platform outsourced workers. It is significant restructuring of domestic manufacturing supply chains will greater reliance on suppliers and subcontractors. In addition, the potential growth of on demand outsourcing work as well as other forms of job fragmentation. It causes this question: How outsourced workers are multiple forms of income generating work to achieve economic security and how outsourcing workers can build career across jobs and over time.

Firm in every sector of the economy contract with other firms as part of their production process, as do governmental entities. The functions that are outsourced vary widely. For example: human resources ans research and development functions, building services, recycling, regulation and compliance, accounting, credit card collection, call centres, mortage and check processing, information technology and data processing, logistics and transportation, machine maintenance, cable installation, food services, food processing, parts manufacturing and assembly, laundry and housekeeping etc. outsourced jobs causes.

Whether what business impact of outsourcing will be caused? Nowadays, IT outsourcing was clearly a part of an effective management strategy that the companies felt IT outsourcing strategy can bring to achieve positive results. Information technology outsourcing providing servicers will be predicted to provide services that is expected to raise over the next five years minimum. The companies demand clients expected benefits of IT outsourcing and determined that cost reduction, increased operation, efficiency and improved IT effectiveness. What are the impacts of outsourcing to influence better long-term improvement in the business performance? It is impossible to being benefits of significant reduction and lower growth in sellings, general and administrative expense to IT outsourcing company demand clients. Also, pre-existing corporate cultures are focused on business improvement to IT outsourcing company demand clietns. In the past researches, some economists indicated that points can be used to reflect the actual numbers increase or decrease in percent. However, their prior researches shows that prior to outsourcing, the annual growth in selling, general and administration expenses of eompanies in the study was already 4.2 points lower than sector medium. Moreover, within one to two years after IT outsourcing these companies improved even most. Annual growth in selling and general administrative expenses for them was 9.9 points lower efford to assist any IT outsourcing will have selling and administrative expenses for long term. Also, almost two-third of the companies studied outperformed in increased growth in return on asset two to three years after IT outsourcing commenced. Prior to outsourcing, the annual ROA growth rate for companies in the study ws 7.5 points lower than the sector median. After outsourcing, however these companies experienced 8.6 points higher median a substantial change of 16.1 points. Also, nearly two to third of the companies studied grew earnings faster than their peers. Two to three years after IT outsourcing, companies experienced an annual rate of growth in earnings 11.8 points higher than the growth rate of the sector median. Thus, it seems IT outsourcing can assist the IT outsourcing demand clients to reduce expenditure and to raise income both as the same time. Then, it will cause these questions to IT outsourcing demand clients. Is outsourcing influencing in an economic downturn to finance sector in the short term? Is the finance sector's renewed change for outsourcing just a temporary cost-cutting measure? Will today's economic climate initiate long term financial and productivity gains? Whether what are benefits and disadvantages of outsourcing finance sector IT. I shall demonstrate why outsourcing open source software support and maintenance can be a good choice to start. Firstly when company plans to budget cuts expenditures, IT outsourcing is often the first choice. For example in 2003 year, Zurich Financial services' sprawling IT department consisted of more than 7,500 employees. After posting a record loss of 3.4 billion the year before, Zurich decided to cut down on in those staff and outsource nearly half of its IT work. Outsourcing has successfully cut costs by 45 percent and cut the number of in house IT staff by 60 percent. Here are some of the benefits that companies enjoy when they outsource information technology functions to competent, reliable vendors.

In fact, it can be too expensive to maintain, company's own information technology, especially during a recession. Fortunately, many IT functions can be easily and efficiently outsourced, positively impacting individual company's bottom line. Employee costs are much higher than just salary and benefits, keeping employees happy, productive and busy takes time, effort and money. Although, many IT staffs will be dismissed, it will increase the unemployment ratio in societies. But, moving an IT service out of house means financial organizations don't have to worry about technology refresh costs in the future. It also cuts down on human resources requirements, specialist IT service provides which can provide the newest technologies and deliver quality service more than company itself in house information provides are the most effective to develop and implement and upgrade their clients' software or the launch on a new platform, due to the expert's time is wasted on day-to-day duties for whose other IT outsourcing demand clients. However, instead of IT outsourcing service outsourced offshoring in that service sector, how economic impact to influence the outsourced offshoring country. For example, United States continues to run an international trade surplus in services. Many Americans are particularly concerned about the loss of skilled, well paid jobs in such fields as computer programming and accounting etc. positions. These jobs seemed relatively secure at a time when many manufacturing jobs were being cost to import competition. Similarly, telephone call centers, once viewed as an esonomic development opportunity in some areas, increasingly are moving low wage countries, such as India and the Philippines. Thus, offshoring raises many questions for policymakers and general public. For example, which service jobs will be affected most by import competition. What are the likely effects of service-sector offshoring on U.S.A. output, employment and our standard of living, such as America? Is offshoring really a problem that requires restrictive government actions or are other kinds of policies more appropriate to give Americans or other countries the highest possible living standard?

The term of offshoring refers to the relocation of jobs and production to a foreign country. The relocated jobs and production could be at a foreign office of the same multinational company or at a separate company located abroad. In constrast, the term outsourcing doesn't necessary imply that jobs and production are relocated to another country. The major outsourcing service jobs include human resource, accounting and information technology etc. in-house service jobs in large organizations. However, the loss of service jobs and factory production is caused by offshoring is diffuclt to measure. It is also difficult to determine the impact of offshoring on total services employment in the United States or other countries. International trade in services covers a wide range of industries and activites. For example, travel and transportation includes travel expenditures, passenger fares and frieght and port services, royalties and license fees cover transactions including patents, copyrights, trademarks and other intangible proprietary rights to use, produce or distribute products. Other private services include many of these industries, such as education, financial services insurance, telecommunications and other professional services etc. Some economists indicated that occupational employment statistics for the Unisted States provided additional evidence that past service sector offshoring had been small. About 14 million service jobs were at risk of offshoring in 2000 year, when about 96 million service jobs had a low risk of ofshoring. The decline in the at-risk service occupations from 2000 year to 2002 year was about 218,000 jobs or roughly 109,000 jobs annually, relatively small number that is consistent with the estimates of McCarthy or Zandi. In percentage terms, employment in the at risk occupations fell at a faster rate from 2000 year to 2002 year than in the low risk occupations. This faster decline is consistent with offshoring activity, although the decline is consistent with other explanations as well, such as faster of technological change in industries employing the risk occupations or greater cyclical sensitivity in these industries. Because offshoring was not the only cause of job loss in the risk occupations, the number of jobs moved offshore was undoubtedly less than 109,000 jobs annually. However, the estimates may understate the total impact because domestic companies with expanding worldwide employment may have located may of their newly created jobs abroad even when they didn't reduce their US employment. Some of those foreign jobs might provide services to US customers and potentially foreign jobs might provide service to US . Conversely, the estimates may overstate the total job loss from offshoring of the foreign outsourcing of some support jobs prevents the loss of other domestic jobs by keeping US firms competitive in world markets. For example, cost reductions from offshoring IT jobs might help a US financial services company win foreign contracts, preserving many professionals and support jobs in the US.

Lower production costs in foreign countries are a major cause of service sector offering. Although, the costs of land and other resources may be cheaper abroad, but the main difference betweeb the US and developing countries is labor costs. There is a large gap in computer programmer wages between the US and other countries. Any organizational capital includes both physical capital, such as machinery and computers and human capital , such as skills and knowledge. The cost savings is come from offshoring also might be reduced if the firm needed to pay higher transportation and telecommunication costs or management spends more time on service quality and data security. Still, the much lower levels of wages ans benefits in developing countries suggests that many services can be produced abroad at lower cost. The in-house professional relocation of labor-intensive service activities, such as legal transcription services to countries with lower labor costs is consistent with economists' basic theory of international trade, comparative advantage. So, in-house outsourced professional service will be a corporative advantage, if the country's legal profession is poor level to compare with the another country. e.g. the skill in-house the legal professional labors of the developing country, such as China is poor educational level to compare with the developed country, such as US. So, if China large organizations chose to outsource themselves in-house legal service jobs to outsource offshoring to US legal professional lawyers to do. It can bring comparative advantage to China large outsourced in-house legal service organizations, due to these China outsourced large organizations can reduce to employ to pay too much salaries to these many in-house Chinese domestic lawyers and the US outsourced legal consultants whose can give more professional legal recommendation to serve to the China large organizations.

In conclusion, although offshoring strategy can increase unemployment chance for this disadvantge. But, all of outsourcing benefits weighs are more than the offsourcing disadvantages. However, outsourcing strategy can have these benefits to the outsourced service demanders. Such as outsourcing is no longer just about cost saving, it is also a strategic tool that may power the twenty first century global economy. Moreover, outsourcing can increase productivity and competitiveness, e.g. for every 1000 jobs British Airways sends to India , the airline saves $23 million, companies can devote a portion of their outsourcing savings to helping employees make job transitions, also leader can no longer afford to view outsourcing as a business tactic, it is now essential to remain competitive. On the world stage, workers now compete globally, so individuals must continually learn more to vie successfully with their peers worldwide, the average company only spends about 20% of the value of its outsourcing contracts to manage its relationship with the outsource provider. So, in the positive view point, outsourcing strategy can bring a potential primary driver of the global economy development. Although, outsourcing can also cause the raising of domestic unemployment chance. But companies may soon be more outsourced than in sourced, signifying a fundamental reorganization that will affect employees, managers, customers and executives. Customers' choice will increase product costs will drop and workers' roles will change. Finally, the most important, the developing country will earn comparative advantage from the developed country's employers' offshoring jobs provision. Thus, the developing country's unemployment rate will be reduced, then the global economy will be kept more balance fairly.

Reference

Abrahamson, E., & Rosenkopf., (1993). Institutional and competitive bandwagons: Using mathematical
modeling and a tool to explore innovation diffusion.
Academy of management review, 18(3), 487-517.
Hill, C.W.L. & Jones, G.R. 1995. Strategic management, An integrated approach. Boston: Houghtom Mif In.

CHAPTER EIGHT

Internet Multi-Level Marketing saving cost strategy

●

What are the differences between multi level
marketing and direct personal sale?

It seems that multi level marketing (MLM), netwrok marketing and direct sellers scheme marketing which are under the pyramid retail sales criterion. It means only third parties with no connection to the selling organizations are considered legitimate "ultimate users". Consequently, it deems the consumption of product by distributors (participants), "internal consumption" to be illegalitimate and simply a cover for fraud.

As multi level marketing or direct sellers from pyramid schemes both marketing which need individual participant or distributor who give money to buy their products to join to whose business to earn commissions. It seems the participant or distributor will be client role more than member or business partnership role. So, it seems MLM or direct sellers from pyramid schemes which main income sources are come from participants or distributors (internal clients). Rather, the key question is to determine whether the purchasers, whoever who may be actually resell or consume their products if the sales transactions are thus reveals to legitimate, as a matter of economic principle. They are also revealised to have increased social welfare. By accepting and adopting without further inquiry the "retail sales criterion", even though it is contrary to basic principles of economics and logic. Consequently, I shall indicate these above proposed test to distinguish legitimate from fraudulent enterprise of legitimacy to multi level marketing or pyramid schemes direct sellers both sale channels.

The reasons of legitimacy to multi level marketing or pyramid schemes direct sellers include which are inappropriately not just the consumer surplus flowing from, but also the profits that the parent firm earns from selling products to dustributors for their internal consumption. This error is caused by asserting that the resulting biased estimates of cash flow are sufficient to indicate that either a pyramid scheme (multi level or direct personal sale) is in progress. These both network sale channels discard all profits earned with internal consumption and because they assume, without the justificaton or validation, that all participants (distributors) in a direct selling enterprise act to as to maximize their cash income. What is the mean of relating high rate at which individuals are to direct selling is sufficient to be defrauded. It is alternative explanations for the rate at which individuals quit direct selling (the "quit rate"), and it provides no economic analysis or inquiry as to the quit rate those distributors might exhibit outside direct selling. It implies the quit rate of distributors in either direct selling or multi level (network) enterprise is pyramid scheme comparable to what one might observe in the counter-factual in which those individuals are employed as wage labour.

As the accounting theory view, pyramid multi level marketing fraud is considered of circumstances unrelated to pyramid fraud, such as calculations of distributors (participants) income whether a parent company's current cash outflows are fully funded by inflows. More direct personal sale or phyramid theme sale business calculations in this regard are biased toward finding fraud because which discard all profits earned with internal consumption and because which assume without theoretical justification or validation that all participants in a direct selling enterprise act as to maximize their cash income. Alternative explanation for the rate at which individuals quite direct selling the quit-rate and provides no economic analysis might exhibit outside direct selling. In fact, a high rate is sufficient to conclude that distributors (participants) were defrauded is apparent upon noting that there are also high quit-rates in other undeniably legitimate businesses. A direct selling (pyramid) of only a few distributors are able to build businesses that six and seven figure annual incomes is similiarly. Chief Executive officer and the distribution of salaries at many commercial entities exhibits a pyramidal form that logic would conclude that all corporations must be considered pyramid fraudsters in the labour market. Even of an economic analysis is well intentioned from direct personal sale market or pyramid enterprises in any countries. The politicies of different countries governments advocated and other misinterpretations, impose costs on consumers, producers and society at large. An objective appraisal of the costs and benefits with using test that are generated false positives represents the first step toward a meaning ful; analysis of the appropriate public policy.

This direct personal sale or pyramid direct sales scheme is concluded by providing an examination of the costs and benefits of regulation and increased enforcement. It seems direct personal sale market has no any legal doctrine support that only sales to third parties constitute legitimate business activity and application of logic and the misinterpretation and misapprehension of prior court rulings that have biased inquiries into the potential to generate false positives. So, some economists have failures of logic and economic that have characterized prior evaluations of public policy low and pyramid schemes or direct sale market.

Our goal is to providing some guiding principles to indicate economically sensible, how a true pyramid scheme or direct personal sale market can be identified and the costs and benefits of different approaches as to how fraud should be detected, with MLM and pyramid direct sale schemes. Otherwise, Multi level market, MLM compensates not only in the form of commissions on sales to distributors (participants), but it also compensate commissions on the sales of it's recurits. The fact, that the share prices of MLM enterprises that have one public have remained positive indicates that the market believes MLM enterprises have value and that this value will be sustained. In constrast, a direct personal sale market enterprise is unsustainable, e.g. a pyramid scheme that will collapse. Or always faces the threat of being shut down as a fraud by regulators, would not be able to sustain positive market value.

It is important to note that legitimate multi level network direct selling benefits not just the parent firm and distributors, but also businesses and society at large. A MLM's products may require its salespeople to invest meaningful time and effort in educating the client as to the benefits of the product, resulting in a long sales cycle before sale is concluded. MLM provides the opportunity to every participant (distributor) to build to personal networks to introduce potential purchases to products. As a matter of economic principle of revealed preference or revealed profitability. Similarly, consumers who choose to purchase from legitimate MLM network direct sellers, they perceive more value in purchasing from a direct seller relative to other alternatives.

Many distributors join the MLM to purchase a preferred product at a lower price. Other distributors find MLM is a convenient way of support their income on their terms and according to their needs, for example by working why reasonally or part time. Another participants may find that participation in a entry point into a center or business opportunity to invest in their human capital and to acquire a network of business connections. Other participants may find that MLM (network selling) is the perfect match for their talents and skill sets. The goodwill to MLM is needed to concern. Consequently, consumer protection efforts have focused on identifying. Because, same MLM enterprises pretend to be legitimate direct sellers, such as fraudsters' debase the goodwill are trust that legitimate direct selling has established with consumers. Resultly, the direct personal sale enterprises pretend to do legitimate business activities to influence the unhealth or poor economic growth in societies. Otherwise, the Multi level market (MLM) or network market enterprises can do more legitimate business activities to influence the health or poor economic growth in societies.

However, muli level marketing , MLM is as a very popular business model in the Western countries. It is a kind of the method of distribution of products. The method of building a sales network, it is one of the safest carries a very low risks ways of conducting business activity. The enter is to any markets, it is usually with market entry barriers and huge capital needs. Lack of expansion and lack of awareness of common practices. In the traditional business model, the risk of failure is very high. Also, unknown is the uncertain concerning the return on investments. However, despite high level of risk, this is the most popular business model.

So, multi level marketing is also called "network marketing". It is one of the fastest developing and still the least understand methods if introducing products to the market. It is mainly due to poor understanding of the system that multi level marketing is often regarded as network sales, pyramid sales or even pyramid schemes. It is marketing strategy and way of functioning of a company and its partners' independent distributors. Multi level marketing is a branch of direct sale. It involves offering products and services directly to clients on the basis of individual contacts, usually at direct's home, workplace or in other locations outside permanent retail sale branches. It is a form of sale outside, a traditional ship chain. It allows sellers to build personal structures of partners, who provide additional commissions from their sales. Every seller in multi level marketing has an opportunity to build own structure of salesman in which everyone is rewarded based on the marketing plan valid for each company. At the same time, achieving higher earnings, it is as a marketing strategy, way of functioning of a company and a system allowing to build individual network for independent distributors, classifying it has a branch of direct sales is a big mistake.

What is it's differences to pyramid scheme, MLM or network market and direct personal sale method? First, MLM is a retail sale, which is the most basic form of distribution carried out by means of a retail branch, e.g. grocery shop, chemist's shop department store, online auction site. Second, direct personal sale method is covering ususally the sale of insurance, kitchen wave houses etc. products. In this model of distribution commission from sold products goes only to the seller, who can't build network of his distributors. In order to sell products or services offered by a particular company, who has to be employed in the company as a sales representative. This means that who works for the owner of a company, the company's whose employer, thus the sales representative doesn't work for whose own benefit as in case of personal direct sale marketing. Third, direct personal sale marketing is transferring a product or service from the producer of service provider to the consumer. Otherwise, MLM, Multi level marketing is as a system of rewarding people who contribute to sale of products or provision of services. In the multi level marketing method people contributing to sale are those who recommend a purchase directly from a particular company. The employee whose is provided in course of making an order is rewarded for a recommendation resulting in actual sale, as the bonus system is usually multi level and allows generating passive income, income is not the direct effect of the work of recommending person. This works, this way is as every person has the opportunity to build individual consumer distribution structurer. In order words, multi level system rewards for directly recommended persons and recommended directly by direct ones. Fourth, MLM, it means mail order sale, this kind of distribution is characterized by lack of retail points in which products could be exchanged for money. The client makes an order directly in the company after learning about its offer on television, in telephone conversation or from a received catalogue. Finally, direct personal sale method is an illegal organization of sales, which is often mistaken for muti level marketing. One of the main reasons for an illegal organization is presented as a multi level system. The difference that makes pyramids illegal and multi level making legal is the inability to distribute a product or provide service. If there are no sales of a product, it is impossible to take about marketing companies by promising high sales convince participants to pay high one off about of money that allows then to participate in the programme which makes it impossible for participants to generate sales, as all payments go to the account of those organizing the business. Thus, direct personal sale is nothing like multi level marketing or network marketing . MLM, in which sale is always based on a product or service and the commission system rewards participants depending on the contribution, regardless of held position. So, MLM, it is a network created based on contacts and ties between people and the participation of all members of the network in this activity.

Whether multi levelmarketing can assist economic growth.

We can view multi level marketing from two perspectives, one of them is the point of view of concept, the producer or the company for which multi level marketing is one of possible ways of introducing a new product to the market bearing huge cost with promotion and without the need to transfer rights to a product to someone. The second perspective is the point of view of an independent distribution for whom multi level marketing is a model of business which doesn't require a concept or bearing the risk with investing capital, as in case of typical business activity or franchising, such an approach makes it possible to define MLM as method of distribution of products, in which costs associated with advertising and marketing are covered at the moment of actual sale. Sales are fueled by clients of the MLM company who use their contacts to recommend the purchase of particular products. The MLM company rewards the recommending person with a commission calculated based on the company's marketing plan for a recommendation ending with actual sale. Any marketing plan creates the possibility to generate unlimited revenues and at the same time eliminate risk with the necessity to invest substantial capital required to launch typical business activity.

How Multi level marketing can assist socio-economic development. For example, insurance business is a kind of MLM business, whether it can assist socio-economic development for long term. In insurance sector, insurance companies are looking for innovative methods to spread the message and maximum business in the short time. Many local MLM companies having quite large spread in the market with leading insurance brands to promote their insurance products along with their own products. Insurance sector makes available long time debt for the economic development of the country. At the same time, the MLM route provides employment opportunities and enhances their social status. The MLM members have opportunity to develop themselves personally. This multipe rise of MLM companies can be looked at as a social contribution and these insurance MLM companies or cooperatives are as a development oriented social movement. How insurance sector can assist the economic and social impact of MLM as a tool which can influence society through employment generation, mobilzing long term funds and improving quality of life of people. There has opportunity to attractive propective candidates to gain network marketing companies. Past studies indicated the fact that a 100 % annual turnover rate among sales personnel in certain network marketing company is not unusual. According to the Direct Selling Association in th United States, it indicated 70% of the revenue from the direct selling industry was generated by network marketing companies and most of this come from the better known companies, such as Amway, was multi level instead of single level compensation plans. Such as India, network marketing was in India during mid 90 year was followed by the establishment of the Indian arm of Amway corporation The total turnover of network marketing companies in India was estimated at $30,104 rising in 2005 year with an annual growth rate of 25%.

It seems Amway can assist USA Government to earn much taxation income and sale income to reduce USA unemployment rate. As, Amway exports to India market. Indian Direct Selling Association (IDSA) facilitates membership to build network marketing companies. So, India is a good network marketing for Amway MLM company. However, consumers often have negative perceptions of direct selling organizations and network marketing organization in particular. The aggressive selling techniques, exaggeration of facts in network marketing organization recruiting and pyramiding scams together toward a basis for this negative perception. Network marketing is a subset of direct selling and is also known as multi level marketing structure marketing or multi level direct selling. Network marketing can best be described as a direct selling channel that focuses heavily on its compensation plan because the distributors (members of the networks) may receive compensation in two fundamental ways. First, sales people (distributors) may earn compensation from their personal sales of products and services to the consumers (non-member of the network).

Second, they may earn compensation from sales to purchase from those persons whom who have personally sponsored or recruited into the network (down lines), these down lines continue sponsoring or recruiting to the network sharing the benefits with their sponsors or recruiters (up lines). So, the aim of MLM network market which reward sales agents for buying products and selling products and finding other agents to buy and sell products. In common, the agents (distributors) or participants can earn marketings ranges from 20% to 50% of sales income. In addition, distributors can also receive a monthly commission for their personal volume which is the value of every product who personally buy or sell. Further, the distributors also receive a net commission on the sales of those who recruit into the networks. It seems that the sales developed network marketing are not developed from sales created by retailing, but also developed through recruiting or sponsoring independent distributors. Thus, as distributors continue to recruit or sponsor not distributors to expand whose network, the new distributors will contribute new sales to the network and gain commission in return. This hunge incentive makes the investment in insurance very attractive for a member. For example, coverage margin on first premium for insurance policies can earn the range of 30% to 40%. This given the leverage for structuring the insurance sale through MLM. MLM is a marketing function in which sales people are paid for their personal contribution as well as for the persons who recruit in to the function or process. Employees or sales people who are individual team to work from which who get a reward on the achievement sale force. So, who can sense much ideas to help marketing organizations to raise high demand when demand is too high and the current employees can't meet those are recruits come in the till the position. So, employees are encouraged to bring many employees to the organization.

MLM is also a very important function in providing jobs for the jobless. The recruitment process looks for young jobless people and earns them on income from which who can support themselves. It is happy feeling to know that you are working and at the same time providing opportunities for the loss fortunate to support them. You have chance to increase your paid if you introduce someone to work as participant or recruit or distributer role to any MLM market. It will reduce the numbers of unemployment of the insurance company in society. The idea presents people with great and better learning of the MLM strategy. When people are recruited in to the business, who are trained about its functions. This training acts as a good way of future advancements in the field. It also helps those individuals to use the knowledge to their advantage once who leave to job to enter marketing or sale career.

The job presents flexibility in hours work. Due people can work at any time who feel fits in them schedule. It can also train them to learn how to achieve whose sale target and attempt to do own business and no and captial spending. Is network marketing or multi level selling marketing as it is called all about getting rich quick with minimal effort? Multi level marketing or network marketing means referring products or services directly to consumers within your network. It involves building a network. For each referral is made by the network. The preceding link or upline as those individuals are called in network marketing terms, gets a certain percentage of commission. MLM, network marketing doesn't need you to be a user of the product or service that you would eventually be referring within your network. Network marketing or MLM only need you put ability to put in lots of hard work. In fact, twice as much as in a regular job or business, willingness to learn new diversified skills, ability to discipline your ability to be as network with like minded people who can help you. So, MLM can help unemployment people to find either freelance or temporary or permanent kinds of position choices, such as sales person or distributor role in MLM company. So, network (MLM) marketing can offer various benefits to them like, lower initial costs of setting your business excellent training and product/service knowledge from industry experts, opportunity to earn additional residual income with a greater chance to move into a full time earned income model, flexibility to work at your own pace and time choice of retiring whenever you want.

Network market can be kind of multi level marketing. As network marketing is confronted with a number of issues that include the continuous erosion of campaign effectiveness, the fragmentation of traditional markets, the disappearance of the vendors' information advantage and significant changes in the distribution channel. Based on established building blocks of marketing and social network theory, a conceptual framework called network theory to integrate the two fields in a systematic way.

The networked marketing framework provides a structure for identifying the customer social network's impact on the marketing effectiveness in the different customer lifecycle phases and suggests the use of certain tools to acqire knowledge about the nature and the functional details of the social influence. However, the network marketing framework was tested in a setting on an international sample of a large company's customer database. How customer social network activity with an impact on marketing is the most intense in the purchase phase and the least. Hence, in the awareness phase, as well as the fact, that product and communication are the mix areas most impacted by social networks. For example, health care is an individual necessity and kind of national luxury product of a kind of multi level decision models. Due to health care is neither a necessity or a luxury, it is both since the income elasticity varies with the level of analysis. With insurance, individual income elasticities are typically near zero, when national health expenditure elasticities and commonly greater. It is to expected that measured income elasticities will differ for an individual, a risk-pooling group, or a national health system, just as price elasticities for individual, firm and market demand normally differ from each other. In past, some economists indicate income elasticity of individual, health expenditures under insurance (usually 60% to 95% of total spending) is typically near zero or negative, when the elasticity of national health expenditures with respect to national income is typically greater than 1.0. So, it seems individual income level and health factor has close relationship to decide to buy any health insurance policies.

Whether how multi level decision model quickly resolves to make evident the role of social and private insurance in linking micro and macro analysis in health economics. Within an insurance group, the bulk of the health resources will be allocated to those individuals who are ill and to get benefits from medical care. Individual budget constraints and ability to play concerns are pooled insurance financing. The contrast between the behaviour of the average individual, and the behaviour of the group to buy medical health insurance mean is well illustrated by insurance. However, medical health insurance pools are not only likely to display separation between group and individual behaviour, who are designed to bring about such a separation. The purpose of medical health insurance is to remove the individual budget constraint, and to reduce or eliminate the influence of cost of care on patient's and physician's decisions of how much care to use. If persons are fully insured, correlations with measures of individual income provide no information about income effects per each, e.g. the effect of monetary budget constraints, but instead reflect the influence of other unmeasured variables, cost of time, family resources, education, preferences etc. that are correlated with an individual's income. Hence, it seems that multi level model of determinants of pyramid or network sale method is suitable to sell in health insurance market. In any country's health insurance market, it will have two kind groups of people who will feel who have need to buy health medical insurance product. One group is without purchase any health medical insurance product , and another group owns health medical insurance product . At the macro level, income effects are still strong to influence anyone to decide to buy health medical insurance product, but variation factor due to differences in health status can also influence anyone to decide to buy health medical insurance product . With the country's people who feel need of health medical product, the pooling of funds will remove the insurance market income constraints and tends to strengthen the correlation of individual health status with expenditures. However, individual income effects still dominate the insurance market in the health medical insurance any country. So, it seems that health medical product insurance will have large share to lead to any country's insurance product income among of the travel insurance, accident insurance, life insurance, car insurance, employee welfare insurance etc. different kinds of insurance products market in any country. So, mulit level marketing shall be suitable to enter insurance product sale market.

Direct sale represents a modern product distribution system directly to consumer. Generally, directly to their homes, to their workplace or other places, besides retail shops. Ths best known type of direct sale, the network marketing or multi level marketing implies the existence of a network of distributors which earn income from selling on commission, to which who add the trade marketing. So, insurance, travel agent, share broker, property agent etc. these occupations which can belong to multi level or network marketing.

Following, I shall discuss the another kind of multi level marketing, e.g. franchise business. Franchise means the field of activity in which it was used. It is a license allowing the designee to sell and market a company's products or services in a particular place, using the name or the trade mark of the company, e.g. Mc Donald fast food restaurant. It allows whom to do business for the franchise owner, but not through the franchise owner. From the marketing point of view, franchise represents a distribution system based on the partnership between two parties which are legally independent. Between the franchisor (the proprietary owner, the owner of the trade mark of products and services) and the franchisee. However, developing a franchise using a well known trade mark, so it is a more complex distribution system in multi level marketing view point. Also, franchise business can be sold from internet sale channel in the multi level marketing technological view point.

●

Why the internet has positive influence on direct sale industry in multi level market to assist economic growth.

However, an important factor for increasing the turnover generated by direct sale companies and multi level marketing network represents a structure that is continuously changing. As technological changing, internet invention can raise the MLM sale method of chance. In multi level sale marketing, as house agent or franchise sale agent, insurance agent, share agent etc. these kind of occupations who can expand their businesses market from internet. Some of the trends indicate strong growth multi level products in international market. Also, high participation of women in multi level marketing, women are begining to realize that the internet makes it possible for them to reinvent themselves and begin a multi level business that requires little risk and low start up cost, such as internet sale method, these are no age limit to develop the multi level internet sale channel business and internet sale business can be an important market shares for household products in multi level marketing globally.

Besides these trends, the internet has positive influence on direct sales industry. Internet has had an impact in relations between direct seller and the company and between the direct seller and the consumer. The main multi levels through which the internet helps the development of multi level sale industry. Due to the internet has allowed direct sellers and customers to maintain contact outside the face to face meetings, it also allows direct sellers can use blogs and social media page to sell whose products, direct sellers can use electronic mailings and have online access to products and services brochures, the customers can pay to buy any online products through internet banking conveniently, more and more people were extended his professional activities of direct selling through the use of the internet and social networks, a direct selling activity can be run from home and doesn't require a high investment. Some may even give follow up orders by electronic means.

From the seller's point of view, the major attraction of direct selling is that internet sale channel offers an equal and flexible income opportunity to men and women, across all ages, level of experience and social origins. In the multi level marketing view point, the direct selling industry development trends will be direct influence by maintaining these advantages for the distributors and by using and developing the communicating modern technologies. So internet sale channel will be the potential multi level marketing to influence how to distribute products or service and to through direct sales and mulit level marketing are determined by a set of economic technological and even social factors.

●

Whether multi level marketing can influence economic growth in poverty countries.

I feel that the role of multi level marketing in poverty countries to influence economic growth is important. For example, some businesses who need to manufacture and sell whose products to clients directly. So who need to set up factories and to open shops in local and overseas markets. It seems who need to exploit and save many investors loading more minimal amounts to prepare to sell immediately. It will raise recruiting new downlines and high cost of products as well as who also need to establish production plants in themselves countries or foreign countries to exploit local or overseas economics and to reduce the numbers of unemployment, among many other benefits. It seems the role of multi level marketing can reduce poverty countries unemployment ratio from internet sale channel, e.g. online salesperson , delivered products service and website design technician or computer technician etc. different website related positions will be created to sell to any online buyers conveniently from online sale channel.

Multi level marketing, e.g. online sale channel method can assist any country's businessmen to sell whose products to overseas easily. So, multi level marketing is one global sale market. Such online businesses that empower the people by providing opportunities to the first time businessmen to start businesses to sell their products to overseas market from internet (online sale) channel easily in the beginning. Moreover, multi level marketing has the potential of being a good source for job creation, income generation to sell products to any countries' buyers from online sale channel by websites contact conveniently at their homes.

Whether multi level marketing can solve poverty challenge. If multi level marketing deliberately target the poor as recruits, what role does multi level marketing play in income generation? Is there any relationship between MLM and job creation? Does multi level marketing (MLM) lead to skill and personal development of MM distributors? There are several appraches to poverty challenges. Examining them provides a necessary understanding of the nature of poverty. There are five main approaches to cause poverty challenge: The economic growth, the basic needs of rural development, the target and employment creation approaches. First, the economic growth approach would be leaded to distribution of income by the participation of the poor. In fact, economic growth need long time to develop in any countries. Also, multi level marketing, e.g. online sale channel needs a long time to build online buyer numbers to sell to different countries from distributors' websites globally. It seems this online sale method can assist global economic growth to give benefits to the developing countries to poverty people to solve unemployment challenges during any online businessmen build their websites to sell any products for long term. So, solving poverty challenge is needs long term time to develop any country's economy growth. Multi level marketing can be one of online sale method to solve unemployment challenge to poverty countries globally. Second, the rural development approach recognizes that poverty is multi dimensional. Thus, it aims at providing basic necessities of life, such as food, clean water, shelter, education, health care, and employment to rural dwellers in general. However, the limitation of this approach is that it doesn't directly target the poor. Again, decisions on rural areas to target may be done from political motives. Third, Target approach specifically aims at certain groups in the implementation of poverty programs, e.g. provision of social safety nets, micro credit and school meal programmes etc. Finally, employment creation approach emphasises the need to eliminate unemployment and underemployment. This will be achieved by creating employment from online sale channel.

The whole concept of multi level marketing is relatively new to any European and Western countries where which have existed for long term. For example, the DVD disc is a conglometrate of all firms that distribute to buyer contact in location away from fixed areas, like retail stores particularly at home. It is the locational characteristic that distinguishes it from other forms of personal selling. Multi level marketing is a subset of the DVD disc distributors are used in selling company products and also in recruiting other distributors. As a result, they receive compensation for their sales and from sales of those individuals who recruit. The senior distributors are called uplines when their recruits are called downlines. Other common products sold through multi level marketing include health and fitness product, cosmetics, cleaning agents, electrical appliances and several others which are popular to sell from this MLM marketing either network market or/and online market both methods.

It is very important to influence many multi level marketing companies do not incur any cost on advertisement since who can use internet to advertise whose products in their websites to let global online buyers to discover after they type the seller's website address to enter their websites at home conveniently. The distributors in MLM are usually organized into networks structure connection. Two main types of such structures are the binary and unilevel structure. The former allows just two direct downlines at each level and the other direct recruits are to be placed at different levels in the network of downlines. On the other hand, the unilevel structure permits the recruitment of an unlimited number of downlines. Direct selling firms usually opt between two choices either employees or independent distributors. There are no salaries or other fixed costs associated with recruitment of independent distributors. So a non selective recruitment used with a straight method of compensation often tends to draw poverty people easily earned incomes from only a modest commitment in time and effort. It seems to commission income method. The recruitment of a new distributor allows for only a single connection. However, double registration of a single distribution is not compatible with the MLM compensation plan. A distributor is allowed to participate in three activites of the MLM company's purchase of the products as users, sale to customers and access to mark up profit and recuritment that expansion of the network occurs. The diffusion of the product or service in the market is stimulated strong by the consumption or purchase of the product.

The benefits to MLM offers to distributors include low start cost, distributors can enjoy from the income of others, e.g. the downlines benefit in the distribution network of online sale to different advertisers can help the distributor to advertise whose products to earn commission income from website; online retail group volume and other bonuses and incentives, personal development via training and business support materials to sell from online sale channel, enhanced enterpreneurial spirit to sell products from onlibe channel globally, improved interpersonal skills and increased self confidence and jobs creation from online sale channel.

Nowadays, estimate that 97% of products are purchased and use consumption, which are consistent with legitimate multi level marketing to earn commission income, e.g. a online sale channel is more than a pyramid sale channel. Many of business operations are consistent with the socially beneficial from MLM model and inconsistent with the socially harmful pyramid scheme model. Applying on economic test that requires member performance payment incentives to be primarily funded out of retail based product sales to be classified as a legitimate MLM, based on prior test, at least 62% of total life or eating product purchases would need to be retail based online sale channel. However, multi level marketing is a mulit million dollar global industry. There exists differentiating a valid mulit level marketing scheme and pyramid money circulation scheme. Multi level or network marketing is a form of business that uses independent representatives to sell products or services to family or friends etc. It is a business strategy, which involves participants at various levels, the level above getting returns at the levels below it. Basically, it works on the principle of duplication to increase retail or sale activity. The survival of the system, depends on the chain of earns commissions from retail sales who makes, and also from retail sales made by other people who recruit.

Direct selling organizations can be of various types, multi level format, network hierarchal structure or the organization can be flat. Multi level marketing activity is a method of distributing products or services in which is from distributrs. MLM has these characteristics: the presence of sponsorship lines that create financial rewards between distributors. Suppose x recruits y, x becomes y's sponsor and distributors. Suppose x immediate upline y recruits z, z who as personal recuits of y, and x are y's frontline people (z, t and u) recruited by same sponsor y and on same level and members of the same generation (z, t and u) sponsorship lines seem like family trees. In fact, these sponsors are often called genealogies. Suppose persons s and y are both recruited/sponsored by x. However, y has been more aggressive, heavily recruiting than s. y will become more financially successful than s, even through they are on the same level and had entered the business together. The higher the sales a group generates, the higher would be the amount of commission received by x. There are numerous recognition levels, for example, Amway has various levels of recognition, each with its own unique title and perks. One begins as a basic distributor, works whose way up through the ranks from silver producer to gold distributor to platinum direct distributor to Ruby direct distributors climbing up the ladder to crown direct distributor to crown ambassador direct distributor. But none of the levels and title is authoritative. In MLM schemes, the uplines are paid commissions and bonus on the sales made by their respective downline members. The company using multi level marketing method is a MLM company. The MLM company can be a firm, an individual corporation or other business entity, e.g. Amway, Mark Kay, Modicare etc. MLM entities. It's features include word of mouth sales, means savings on marketing and advertising costs, company can change their similar products in stores, the technique develops loyal customers who enjoy buying from other people who know. It is such a pyramid scheme " which concentrates on the commissions, the participant could earn just for recruiting new distributors" and which generally ignore the marketing and selling of products and services. Pyramid scheme means any sales device or plan under which a person gives consideration to another person in exhange for compensation as the right to receive compensation which is derived primarily from the introduction of other persons into the sale device or plan rather than from the sale of products or services or other property. Pyramid means a multi layered network of subscribers to be a form by subscribers enrolling one or more subscribers in order to receive any money benefits directly or indirectly, as a result of enrollment. It is similar to a continuous chain of participants or investors is recuited, in which each pays a fee to participate and receives money by recruiting others into the system. So each participant can build multi layered network of individuals to have chance to earn more benefit, if who can distribute products to sell successful from whose downline recuriters network.

Finally, the main question is whether this MLM network sale method can assist any country economic growth. I shall analyze what the difference of social effects (influences) are from these kind of sale methods, such as direct personal sale and auto online sale and multi level (network) sale. A phenomenon appears that the distribution companies accept normal direct personal selling method to cause education expenditure to bring loss their bases of values all at once. It comes a lot of direct sellers are lost to any countries. Due to it raise the compensation to the choice of direct personal sale companies. For example, China government achieves laws and policies to stop direct personal sale scheme companies to enter to local market to sell their products. Because China decides to protect its local businesses benefits to let them have ability to sell their products, due to reducing the number of growing foreign direct personal sale scheme companies exist in China itself country. Although, China will reduce GDP income from foreign direct personal import sale. But it can protect its local businessmen benefits to reduce competition. Otherwise, Multi level (network) marketing is a marketing approach that can motivate its participants to promote a certain product among their friends. It can exist in one form before in the internet age began, such as pyramid scheme. Social networks are everywhere, our email and phone address books, our famil relatives etc. Social network has web-based form, as facebook, twitter, linkedin networks made them more tangible. Moreover, internet can be good sale channel for multi level market, it gives the potential to accumulate small rewards from each participant to a sizable sum, as internet channel can allow advertisers to attract early adopters to earn commissions when the advertisers can help any multi level market companies to sell products successfully from internet channel. So, online advertisers and participants or distributors who can earn profit from multi level marketing. It seems Multi level marketing can give chance to let any participants to buid many downline recruiters to assist the team leader to sell many products from internet channel. So, the team leaders and team members do not need capital to set up their businesses and who can do business with the MLM company together easily from internet channel.

MLM or network market is often compared such as direct sales e.g. insurance, franchises etc. In fact, it is in the nature of pyramid schemes for the money to go to the person at the top of a pyramid of participants, with the majority of participants found to be in a losing position at the bottom regardless of when it collapses or is terminated. So, the compensation plan can be considered product-based pyramid schemes or recruiting MLM's because their compensation plan rewards recruiting of distributors through commission from their purchases more than selling direct to consumers. Distributors must not need to purchase products from the MLM in order to participate in the business. These findings raise some important questions: what kind of business has no clients? Only MLM's pretending to be direct sellers. Who is buying the products that can earn income from different countries residents online sale channel. Only MLM's distributors and advertisers are their main customers. If there are no direct sales to speak of, then who is making profits of these supposed sales. Only MLM company founders and officers. Whether multi level marketing can be potential tool for socio-economic development. For example, insurance business is just one among them. Selling insurance policies can operate from internet channel conveniently, traditionally is considered as a job or business. With the competition raises in industry sector, companies are looking for innovative methods to spread the message and maximum business in shorter time. Many local MLM companies have quite large spread in the market, as joining with leading insurance brands to promise life product policy protection to reduce clients' risk loss from internet MLM sale method. So, insurance sector makes online MLM route provides employment opportunities of people and enhances their social status. This multiple role of MLM companies can be looked at as a social contribution and which can develop oriented social movement.

In conclusion, MLM can raise employment generation, mobilizing long term funds and improving quality of life of people. In traditional, successful personal selling based on referrals is the key to ensure regular expansion of client base and building long term client relation. A country like India offers well run MLM online marketing networks to promote consumer products. Conveniently online MLM marketing may become slow or stagnated over a period of time. Online, Multi level marketing may be the tool in such situation, India has many people, so the online multi level businesses can be built to attempt to operate in this country. Concept selling mostly used personal selling as a tool where the sales people depend on referrals. In MLM technically, e.g. online sale, the promotion expenditures on advertisments channel margins etc. is distributed among the participants as individual product distributors or product advertisers , as who can do online business from commission incentives to build businesses from internet. Hence, internet technology can raise MLM to have competitive advantage. For example, it is common knowledge that MLM works on the concept of time leverage. A work to be done by you 100 days can be completed in one day if you have 100 people under you in a chain doing one days work. You can earn a % of incentive for the work done by each of those 100 people under your team downline. Through it is given various names like network marketing, freelance network chain marketing. To conclude, MLM can assist any countries economic growth to compare other kind of sale methods easily in the short time in possible.

CHAPTER NINE

FM how helps organizations to avoid resource waste

How green building helps organizations to reduce resource waste
green building avoids resource waste
The relationship between organization resource and earth resource in behavioral economic view, global organizations use any kinds of resource, such as office, warehouse facility building resource to build any new offices, warehouses, supermarkets, shopping centers, car parks, whether they can bring global building resources reducing number to satisfy human houses living needs, if one day building resources are facing any kinds building material is reducing number, but global applying steel, wood, brick etc. different kinds of building material number increases, when global population number is still increasingm any high houses' building materials need increase, even low wood houses' wood natural resource needs increase in order to let many people can live in the expensive wood houses. SO, it brings this question: Would wood, natural resource, steel, brick resource have shortage supply challenge, due to office, warehouse, shopping center,manufacturer, ther fixed assets number building need increases, but the same time, global houses need number also increases, when polulation increases? Can businessmen their fixed assets : offices , warehouse, shopping centers, factories, supermarkets, etc. building need bring negative impact to influence future human living house resource nu mber decreases?

I assume that global businessmen their offices, warehouses, shopping centers, hospitals, private school education organizations, supermarkets etc. business organizations their buildings number is sudden increasing high, due to many organizations can earn more profit to expand their businesses. So, they will need to spend much woods, steels, bricks etc. different kinds nature resources to build any high , height offices buildings in different countries. So, wood, steel brick etc. different kinds of offices building material need must also sudden be influenced to sudden increase by global business organizations increasing number. When global businesses organizations number increases, it will cause global high height offices number increases, because every business organizations must need to rent any building office to operate their businesses. If global has many new businesses are continue growing, they will influence offices building need in possibe, even for food business , e.g. supermarke, restaurant building material need will also increase, if the reestaurant can earn more profit, then it will need to expand itself restaurant vacancy floor to let many food customers do not need to spend long queue time to wait table in order to avoid to loss these food customers, even it will buy any shopping center location to build one or more than one restaurant to satisfy food customers need . So building material needs to the new restaurant design, it may decide to decorate all restaurant location, to feel food customers to feel more comfortable when they are sitting in its restaurant.SO, when the restaurant changes its inside design , it needs to find designers to buy any new building materials to design its restaurant to be new one in order to attract food customer choice.

I assume that global many old restaurants need to recorate their inside, or many global restaurants number increases, then any restaurants material natural resource need number may also be influenced to increase. Then, our earth building material resource for restaurants need will influence general office buildings material resource, shopping center building material resource decreases to supply. When, global many restaurants are needed to build, more building material resource is needed to be used build new restaurants or is needed to decorate to change old restaurants design . So, our earth will have much building material resources to be used to build new restaurants or they are be used to decorate the old restaurants design in order to change new restaurants design function. So, our earth building material natural resources for new or old restuarants , which must increase, when global has many restaurants need any kinds of building materials to be used to help them to build new or old restaurants. Then, they must influence natural resources of building material supply number to be reduced to satisfy any office building matierals user need, even any house building material user need, if global offices and houses number sudden increase. Consequently, due to global building material natural resource can not be produced rapidly in order to satisfy any office building, shopping center, house, supermarket etc. different kinds business organizations or private houses needs. Then, the natural resource of building resources shortage, it may influence any kinds of building material production price increases. It may influence global business organizations need to pay high price to rent office or build office, or build supermarket, or build shopping center, even any private houses prices increase, when global building material natural resource has no enough number to be supplied to satisfy builders' need in order to help any office, supermarket, shopping center, supermarket warehouse etc. business organization users to build their properties to operate their businesses. SO, these businessmen must need to spend much money for building expenditure, when they begin to do their businesses. Even, public or private house buyers also need to pay more expenditure to buy houses to live , when any kinds of building material price increases.

So, it explains why global business organizations number increases may influence global public or private houses prices increase, when our earth has no enough natural resource to be building matieral supplied to satisfy global construction properties development need. Finally, when global construction properties developers feel our earth building material natural resource encounters supply shortage challengem due to they need to pay higher price to buy any kinds of building material to help any business organizations to build their offices, restaurants, supermarkets, shopping centers, wareshouses etc. different fixed assets buildings or they need to ehlp any public or private houses buyers to build their houses. Consequently, any one businessmen or house livers must need to pay high price to buy any houses or offices , restaurants, hospitals etc. different buildings either to live or to use for business operations. Hence, it seems that they have chose resource supply surplus or shortage relationship between business organizations and private house buyers.

ON conclusion, I recommend that any business office buildings ought choose green buildings orrice, their advantages may include to avoid nature resource waste, improved indoor environment, quality of life , saving water, reduce , reuse, enhanced health, eco-friendly for life, reducing operational cost and maintenance , energy -efficient, non-renewable, vs renesable resource, keep it clean, protecting our ecosystem . Hence, green buildings can not only reduce or eliminate negative impacts on the environment, by using less water, energy, or natural resources.

Moreover, green buildings, or substainable design, is the practice of increasing the efficiency with wich buildings and their sites use energy , water and materials, and reducing impaction human health and the environments for lifecycle of a building. So, on environmental benefits of grren building aspect, it can enhance and protect bio-diversity and ecosystems , imprive air and water quality, reducing waste streams, conserve and restore natural resources, on economic benefits of green building aspect, it can reduce operating costs, improve occupant productiviity, enhance asset value and profits optimize life-cycle economic performance, on social bebefits of green building aspct, it can enhance occupant health and comfort, improve indoor air quality, minimize strain on local utility infrastracture, improve overall qualty of life.

Consequently, if any organizations can apply green building concept to design and build their offices, waterhouses, restaurants, shopping centers etc. different kinds of business green buildings, even ourselves houses design is chosen by green building concept. On behavioral economic view, green building concept is the best moethod to help us to reduce natural resource waste nowadays. Then, I beleive that our earth nature resources won't be easte easily.

facility management helps organizations to avoid resource waste

Can facility management helps organizations to avoid resource waste? How waste management helps in productivity improvement? Waste management is more long term, which involves investment in new technology processes, product and training that can improve production efficiency and reduce waste in using least amount og materials to make and package the products can reduce the materials ,cost and waste.

Why the facility management of waste dosposal is important? When waste is disposed of or recycled in a safe, ethical and responsible manner, it helps reduce the negative impacts of the environment, ensuring that waste management procedures are carried our with regularly helps ensure the fewer waste materials go to the general waste system. som if any organizations can implement the most efficient facility management system, then it can help the organization's internal any building material to keep long ife time. When the organization can have the best building facility materials , it doed not need to spend much money to carry on repairment. Then, building resource cost must not often changed new, it's fised repairment or building material purchase expenditure must reduce as well as the organization's building materials do not waste easily.

Why does facility management help organization to reduce waste cost? This is because of a company can manage its waste properly, reduction in waste can help the company to reduce its cost. Waste minization is a set of processes and practices intended to help managers to see waste minimisation as a primary focus for most waste management strategies. It can reduce waste and usually much improves resources optimisation. Why is facility management software important for productivity? Can efficient facility management bring efficient resource management for organizations?

For organization, building efficiency is absolutely critical for reducing overhead and contributes directly to corporate green initiatives. Building efficiency also improves the operations of the business as whole, and it ensures that employees are able to work productivity in a comfortable environment. Beside having the potential to directly improve productivity, facility management can influence other of employees' lives that contribute to the overall output of an organization. FM can improve social interaction among colleges as well as enabling them to work in an effective, focuses and motivated manner. So, FM has close relationship to let organizations can use resources efficiently, even avoiding wastes resources ad reduces long term cost. Organizing maintanance, repairs and security of the building and premises. This protects employees and FM in organizations may include: claening offices, handware inspection and maintenance, environment health and safety, space management, efficient transportation space parking resource arrangement, operational efficient resources implemenation . So, facility management and efficient resource has relationship of a multiple disciplines to ensure functinality , comfort, safety and efficiency of the build environment by people, place, process and technology resource management.

Today, many organizaions recognize the importance of FM to efficiently manage its properties . Their data to increase productivity by FM, are heating and coolong tasks carried out efficiently? To meet organizations every day needs, some organizations require spaces , such as meeting rooms, or huddle spaces. Hence, facilities management and corporate real estate provisions are becoming increasing need, on efficient resource management business, goals in the most , effective, efficient are quitable way aspect, FM can optimize and implement solutions which fit the organization's trategic . FM aims to help offices, and building resources facilities empower orgsanizations to function at their most efficient and effective level to use their resources.

From manufacturing platns to healthcare facility boosting efficiency is a goals logistics resource management is important to have proper organizatin policies in plan throughtout every facility. For example, high performance building, are characterized by their efficient use of resources and their ability to enhance the safety, health and productivity. So FM can help organizations to achieve to se resources in high performance effectiveness.

FM can also help organizations to save time. Any organizations must have offices to let employees can work together. If the organization lasks efficient and enough space to let many employees to feel comfortable to work together all working days. Their performance will be caused worse. So, efficient facility management to office rooms spaces, it can let employees to work in the most efficient manner.

What are entertainment theme park intangible resource
How intangible resource excites visitors entertainment need
Amusement , entertainment theme parks aim to provide good playing different kinds of lesiure facilities, and ocean fish performance shows to attract visitors to buy tickets to play lesiure activities when they are staying in the entertainment theme park. I assume that any entertainment theme park must need large lands resources to build the different kinds of entertainment machines facilities to let visitors to choose to play, as well as ocean parks can provide whales animals and human ocean peformance shows to let visitors to see their attraction whales animals performances.

So, enough land supply , it can let the theme park to build different kinds of entertainment machine facilities and ocen park to let many visitors have enough space to stay or walk in the entertainment theme park any time. Even, some theme park builds some hotels to let visitors to live several days, when they can not spend whole day to play all entertainment machine facilities. So, land resources must need , if the theme park needs to increase more different kinds of leisure mahcine facilities, it ought need to expand more leisure machine facilities and let visitors can increase number. So, they won't feel noise and crowd feeling. Because noise and crowd environment may influence some visitors feel discomfortable to enjoy to stay long time in the theme park. Then, it may bring negative lesiure emotion to these visitors.

So, any entertainment theme parks whether their land supply is enough to let it to build more different kinds of entertainment machine facilities and let many visitors can feel the entertainment theme park environment is quiest and not crowd environment factor may influence any visitors' staying time and enjoyment feeling to the theme park, instead of whether its leisure facility activities are attraction. Hence, one attraction land supply to build different kinds of entertainment machine facilities and cean parks and hotels to let visitors can enjoy quiet and not crowd comfortable feeling when they are staying to play any these entertainment facilities inthe theme park.

Entertainment machine facilities will be theme park playing resources, they may include: flat rides, rotter coasters, railways, water rides, dark rides, ferries wheels, transport rides. All of these entertainment facilities their leisure attraction , they may influence lesiure consumer individual enjoyment feeling whether is more or less. So, a theme park is s place with attractions made up of rides, such is roller coasters and water rides. They ususally contain a selection of different types of rides, along with shops, restaurants, and other entertainment outlets.

Theme park cann be enjoyed by adules, teenagers and children. So, a successful theme park must can bring memorable attractions that people want to ride to see over and over again. Great attractions are inclusive and are not overly restrictive. They should have great stroy telling elements and put visitors into unique situations.

Future trends in the theme park industry, they ought concentrate all resources on these aspects: Changes in business models, e.g. it does not consider only entertainment facilities, it ought consider park comfortable environment feeling, e.g. more free, flower, animals, performance, natural environment, more dynamic pricing, changes in interactions between empllyees and guests.So, HRM front line service employee performance will influence whether visitors can feel friendly service feeling (home family feeling), more touchless technology and arificicial intelligence, robots technological resource will be one kind excited entertainment machine facilities to every visitor, they like to play robotic entertainment machines, fresh entertainment enjoyment feeling, more augumented and virtual reality in quest experience, changes in the food experience. So, restaurant food supply resource may bring good taste to excite visitors relas feeling when they feel hungry and they need to find restaurants to eat good taste food.

So, theme park entertainment family resource expenditure must be the highest, e.g. small waterparks can assist less than one million to build, but parks of this size are considered move as water playgrounds. Generally, waterparks , cost between $10 million and $40 million to build, indoor theme parks require on average $10 million to $30 million to build. So, the main resource element is the different kinds of entertainment facilities. Any kind of model of theme park needs to make decision whether which kind of enetertainment facility will be their theme park garden, e.g. water playground or indoor theme park, or natural environment forest enjoyment feeling, ocean park seeing whale performance show etc. theme park kinds. Because capital is limited. So, themem park designer needs to consider whether what kind of theme park feature is the most suitable to build in the land in order to avoid waste building land and not suitable entertainment facilities building material resources, when they can not attract many visitors to buy tickets to enter visit the theme park. For an amusement park example, it is a park that features various attractions, such as rides as well as other events for entertainmetn purposes. A theme park is a type of amusement park that bses its structures and attractions around a central theme, often featuring multiple areas with different themes. The others for amusement park may include: Theme park, carnival, funfair, pleasure ground, safari park, water park.

So, what kind features of theme park construction choice, it may influence future what lesiure needs for the visitors. Theme park investors need to gather fata to make market decision to choose to build what kinds of theme park in order to build what kinds of theme park in orde to attract the kind of leisure choice visitors.

for disney theme park exmample, it avoids birds play the sound in distress. It will there for keep birds away from visitors and allow for guests to eat in peace without being bothered by hungry birds. So, it increases resources for birds only. So, birds can have more gardens to let them to fly. They wont fly away the gardens in Desney. So, any gueses do not feel worry about the sound of birds in distress. Also, any theme parks need to invest resources on safety aspect when any one guest plays any kinds of entertainment facilities, e.g. the safest roller coaster is Blackpool, theme park. It can attract many guests to play its entertainment facilities. This theme park locates near to US one beach. Because , it did not cause any one guest dies before, when they go to US this beach, they will like to pay ticket to play rides entertainment facilities. Because it often spends expenditure on rides repairment aspect, so, it can bring the safest feeling to let any one beach guest feels leisure ride playing need when they visits to this US beach to feel swimming need. They also feel playing rides entertainment needs both. Hence, any kinds of theme park investors need to consider how to allocate limited resources to the different element aspect in order to safety, entertainment facilities attraction , reasonable price, enjoyment animals performance shows, restaurents good food taste providing hotel comfortable living feeling aims to all themem park guests.

CHAPTER TEN

Internet technology resource strategy

Reasons internet is important intangible resource to e-educational organization

Does global resource shortage influence educational organizational resource shortage? For example,global gas resource natural resource shortage, it may influence global gas sale organizations gas product supply number reduced, due to they won't have enough oil raw material to supply to manufacture gas product. So, it seems that they have cause and effect of gas supply and gas product increasing or decreasing price relationship between global oil raw material supply number and gas organizational any kinds of gas products sale number. However, I shall concentrate on discussing whether educational organizational teaching service provision, they will need to depend some resources existence or not, if it is true that global some educational organization will need to depend on some kind of resources, in order to provide their educational service performance more successful. Whether what kinds of resources factor may influence their educational service in success. I shall attempt to indicate examples to explain as below:

Nowadays, global educational service is very competitive. Some countries educational organizations began to apply internet technology to implemenbt distance learning educational service to provide online learning channel to any one overseas student to choose his/her distance learning course to learn. I suppose that internet technology is further learning new trend, it will assist different countries students. They do not need to fly to foreign any one country to learn moew conveniently. SO, they do not need to spend much expenditure to learn from oversea any one university. The expenditure may include air ticket go and return expenditure, foreign living cost, transport cost, food cost, rent cost. Although these distance learning students must still need to pay school fee to the distance learning country, but in fact, when the student chooses to learn from internet channel.

This internet learning channel must help the distance learning students to save much extra not essential living expense. Hence, when the university decides to apply internet technology to provide distance learning courses to let overseas student to learn. The internet technology must be the university's technology resources to keep its any distance learning degree courses, such as undergraduate, master and doctor degrees continue to implement to let any one country student may enjoy to study this overseas university's any high and low degree level courses from internet channel conveniently.

Hence, internet this kind of technology courses may influence whether future any one country's university can continue to implement it's distance learning degrees to let any one country's student to learn. It explains that why the university must need have 24 hours internet service to let global different countries students can follow different daily e-classroom time tables to carry on online learning as well as lecturers can also follow different daily e-classroom time tables to teach their students from online classrooms channel conveniently, hence, the providing distance learning university must need have efficient high speed internet technology facilities to provide e-learn resources to carry on any one classroom teaching service to let any one country's student to feel satisfactory to learn from its e-classrooms. If the university's internet facilities are poor, easy internet linking or rapid internet speed to let many different countries distance learning students to feel its e-classrooms have better performance to compare other distance learning universities competitors. Then, this poor e-classromm learning facilities factor may also influence any one country's distance learning students prefer . So, instead of whether the e-universities degrees courses contents are useful to let distance learning students to feel, whether the e-university's schoolf fees is cheap , whether the e-university's leacturers their past educational experiences, past educational personal quality and effort have more high level, whether the e-university had implemented this online degree course how long time, whether how may distance learning students had graduated for this online degree etc. factor. The e-university's internet technology facility may be one important technology resource factor to influence its anyone e-degree teaching course implement in success.

For this distance learning educational organization case, I assume that although the e-education organization has good educational experience teachers, one good courses design, but if it neglects how to provide excellent internet technology facility to let any one distance learning student to feel its any one e-classroom can provide easy person to person contact learning feeling, e.g. easy listen clealrly to any one e-teacher in any one e-classroom, easy enquires to any one e-teacher in any one e-classroom, easy to see any one teacher or student face in any one e-classroom, easy to communicate to any one e-student in any one e-classroom. Then, its any one different countries' distance learning students may feel its internet service facility can not provide excellent e-classroom leaning channel to let they feel. Then , they may choose another distance learning educational institute to replace very easily. Because any one distance learning student must need to install internet to link to the university's learning website to register to any one e-classroom, if the student's internet can not often link to the e-school's website easily, e.g. in this different learning situation, when one China e-learning student ofren feels that US e-university 's every e-classroom can link to his home's computer only half hour, then the US e-university e-classroom will sudden disappear to the China e-student home computer website easily. SO, the China e-student may feel difficult to learn from the US e-university every e-classroom because he must need to attempt to spend 10 to 20 minutes to click to the US e-university website to register to the e-classroom again. This e-univeristy's university internet sudden stopping linking feeling whcih may influence the China student to feel this US e-university neglects to consider its rapid and easy linking internet technology to let him to continue on learning every time e-course easily. Then, this e-university poor internet linking technology facility it will influence he chooses another US e-learning instirue to replace this US e-learning instirue. It does not considerate matter whether there are many different countries e-students , e.g. above 1000 number, they need to apply themselves homes internet to click to this US e-university's this e-classroom to cause internet internet traffic jam busy to influence any one e-student's home computer webwite can not keep long time internet links to this US e-university , e-classroom at the same time. Although, this US e-university's busy internet traffic jam issue may seem to be one small matter, to compare how to raise any one e-course content design, how to improve any one e-leacturer teaching skill or improve any one e-lecturer teaching skill or quality issues. However, if these different countries 1000 e-students, they have above 500 e-students number, they often feel busy internet traffic jam to influence they can keep long internet linking e-classroom time to this US e-educatoinal institute every day. If this e-course only began three months, they need to spend 20 minutes at least and they need to spend more than one time or more times at least to re link to this US e-university e-clasromm website again. Then, after three months, they can be influenced to choose another US e-education organization to replace this US e-education organization by this US e-school's busy internet traffic jam factor easily. Hence , any one distance learning educational institute must not neglect to consider how to avoid frequent internet traffic jam technology faciliity occurrence problem in order to let global any one e-student does not feel difficult to learn from their e-classrooms. Otherwise, they can choose another elearning institure, it can does not let them to ecounter any internet traffic jam challenge when they need to learn from its any one e-classroom any time.

On conclusion, e-learning internet facility service feeling to every e-student, it may be one kind of intangible technology resource to any one e-educational institute. Because " none any one busy internet traffic jam" e-classroom feeling , which may bring direct positive emotion impact to any one distance learning student to choose continue to learn from this e-education institure or choose another to replace it. So, efficient, rapid, none any busy internet traffic jam technological facility may be the most influential technological resource element to assist any one e-educational institure development in success.

Organization time resource efficient spending methods

Is time limited resource to organizations?

Time is an often ignored but invaluable resource in any organizations. All activities be it procurement, production or product movement involve time within on its own is not measurable unless it is method against time. Time gives a time measure of how an organization performs efficiently and effectively. Is time an organizational resource?

Time is an infinite resource. If not properly managed in an organizatiion, it can have a negative, impact on both employers' and employees' productivity. Organizations should ensure that workers are well equipped to manage time in their duties. So, time is one part to organizational resource , instead of organizational resources are all assets that production process.

The four basic types of organizational resources are human , monetary, raw materials and capital. Organizational resources are combined , used and transferred into finished products during the production process. Hence, time is needed to spend time resources to cooperate other resources, e.g. human resources, financial resources, physical resources and information resources to do any activities, because any organizations activities must need to spend organizational time to carry on any organizational activities. Hence, if the organizations can use its daily time to arrange how different department employees how to work efficiently. Then, the organization can not waste its organizational any time resources within its organization because time is one kind of infinite and intangible organization asset. Any organizations ought not waste its any time resource.

In fact , in any organizations, organizational management views time is as a scarce resource that must be invested as effectively. An organizations time, in contrast, goes largely unmanaged. Although, phone calls, e-mails, instant messages etc. The ability to prioritise and schedule work is extremely desirable for any organization corporate . Indeed, organizations continually overcommit their employers resources. Limiting growth and innovation can be achieved easily, when the organization can manage its time how to use on the best condition, because progress and time tracking is available to support any organizational goal. In organizational studies, resource management is the efficient and the required data are the demands for various resources, forecast by time period into the future as far as is reasonable.

Is a business sense, the term " limited resources" can refer to a training organizations have had to evolve in a climate of how use evaluations to see what needs to change , if the organization feels time is not enough to use, so organizations need to ensure an members of team know their roles are the necessity of delivering on time and budget, seeing how great resource management to software and following resource management. Regardless of the approach and tools used, organizations must determine how to use role-based resources for long-term planning or when the specific resource is not enough to be used.

So, organizations need to learn how resource utilization with busy time/ available time. By establishing effective resource management or predict when inefficiently used resources within the organization and work. Organizational excellence framwwork (performance measurement) by learning and applying these concepts. Organizational any working time is

money and it is best to plan for effective resource, but few organizations treata it thatway number of hours away from their families and friends.
So, any organizations need to calculate " utilization rate", the rate at which a resource is utilize, often used in regard to an employees' time , e.g. for project managers, time management is an essential skill at each of these specific components of time mangement.

CHAPTER ELEVEN

US Space science research organization (NASA) knowledge management innovation benefits

Why does intangible resource may influence NASA organization successurce management strategy

In global space science research industry, it is only one space science research organization in US , this organization establishmenet aims to investigate whether our earth outside has natural resource supplies, e.g. water , air, for example research moon, had been past US apce science research mission, following this US space science research will have unlimited number of any new space science research missions. However, if futuse use sapce science research organization hopes to continue to carry out on researching any new space planets missions in success, e.g. continue researching whether our earth outside has natural resource, e.g. fresh water, air existence in any large, or amll size planets, even their distrances are long away to our earth. Hence, their space science research organization whether it has enough tangible and intangible resources supplying factor as well as how it impkements its resoruce management strategy in order to use resource achieve to carry on researching any new space science research missions efficiently and effectively .

These both issues will be further space scienece research organizaions' main successful factor. So, I shall attempt to explain hw US space science research ourganizaion oughr achieve its resource management strategy in rder to achieve any difficult space science researching missions to be more simple.

NASA was for national aeronautics and space administration NASA to a US government agency that is responsive for science and technology related to air and space. The space age started in 1957 with the launch NASA missions, they are organized work to planetary science, hellophysics, and astrophysics. In NASA organizational structure , the administrators and deputy administrators of NASA are the highest ranked oficials of NASA , the space agency of the US government.

The administrator serves as the senior space science advise of the president of the US . SO, this NASA administrators has authorities to manage their organization;s any kinds of intengible and tangible resources how to be used. However, NASA's organizational structure is based on two primmary levels of managment responsibility. The first is agency management which primarily resides at headquarters. The second is stategic entreprise management which includes managing centers ans programs. so these two departments must have much authorities to manage how any organizational resources to be use for NASA's any space science research missions. However, if they can manage resources efficiently, they can help NASA organiztations to void resources wastes to any further space science research missions . SO, resource management strategy is very important to influence NASA organizations's success or failure, because if it has enough resources to achieve any planned space science research missions, then they can not achieve effectively. SO, resource management strategy is very important to NASA organization.

Global environment protection resource management strategy

On global environment protection resource management strategy aspect, NASA global conserves and protects natural resource through world class habitat and species management programs to our earth natural environment. It reduces the threatened and endangered species by poor natural environment were of ecological , recreational, aesthetic, education and scientific value to the nation's public . The enhancement of the environment, and is a procedural statute for application by the federal agencies.

Hence, NASA organization believes that it needs to learn how to protect our earth natural resource to avoid waste and it brings to influence our earth ecological environment to become more worse. Then, we and our animals can not live comfortable .So, if this most simple protection to our earth's natural environment, NASA can do, then it must have effort to implement the most effective resource management stategy to avoid resource waste or use the least resource to carry on any space science research mission effectively.It seems that how to learn reduce our earth's natural environment resources, NASA can know how to spend or use the least resources to implement any further space science researth missions effectively.

Hence, I feel that NASA is one learning organization, have to help our earth to reducc natural organization waste, even how to manage resources to implement and new space science research mission to be used effectively. It is difficult to general business organizations, they only consider how to earn more profit aim. Otherwise, NASA does not provide effective checks and balances, does not have an independent safety program, and has not demostrated the characteristics of a learning organization. So, NASA is responsible for learning to educate human's fishing or farming businesses can avoid to influence our environment natural resource waste, even it is implemening resource management strategy to save our earth to avoid natural resource waste, e.g. oil, gas protection resource won't have enough supply issus occurrence.

Why does NASA need to be a learning organization?

In fact, learning has always been at the core of NASA 's project management successes and failures. Throughout, its history, the agency and its external stakeholders have conducted periodic studies of the importance of learning from proven best practices in project management. SO, learning effort , it must be NASA organization's intangible resource, it needs have good knowledge management strategy to prepare to learn any new methods to help it to solve any further new space schience resrach mission.

It means that knowledge managagement strategy will ne NASA's effective resource management method. It is only way to help NASA to solve any resource management challenges , when it encounters any difficulties to any space science research missions. Has knowledge management (KM) resource strategy to NASA organization relationship to resource mangement? The KM resources collection is comprised of critical knowledge links and artifacts, instituational knowledge assets, lessos learned from missions and projects, than drive mission success can knowledge management impact to NASA organization's own resource manafement strategy before it implements any space science research missions?

In fact, the benefits of using knowledge managment which may help any organizations, they include improved organization resource manageement effort, better and faster decision making, quicker problem solving , increased rate of innovation, supported employee growth and development , sharing of specialist expertise, better communication, improved business processes. A knowledge management plan is an organized, systematic and focused approach to identifying and implementing the knowledge goals and objectives of a project. So, such as NASA must have many different prepared science research project to be prepared to implement. If it can have good knowledge management plan, used challenges to any one project more easily.

Hence, NASA must need have a good knowledge managment plan, it is organized, systematic and focused approach to identify and implementing the knowledge goals and objectives of any a space science resource project, it is a document for a specific space science research project, department or function, which details. So, NASA needs have effective systems of processes, technologies and roles will be used to manage knowledge withing every space science research mission project.

This, effective knowledge management strategy is the main knowledge management strategy is the main factor to influence NASA organization's further every space science research missions their successes or gailure. It seems that NASA's intangible resource "knowledge management" , it may be the main intangible asset to influence it's any space science research missions whether they can use the least human, money, equipment technology resource to achieve successfully. Even, knowledge management may help NASA organization increase successful rate to achieve any further of different kinds of difficult space science research missions , because when NASA organization can implement an effective knowledge management strategy to learn or improve or revise whether every tim failure to its space science research mission, what are tha main factors to cause their missions failure, e.g. not advanced space technology or space equipment, supplying factor, difficult or not accurate prediction to worse natural space environment, changing factor, not enough skilful training ro any learning time arrangement to one spaceman individual skillful factor, because any one time space science research mission failure, it may due to different not controlled such as space worse changing envioronment or controlled factor, such as not enough learning time to provide to skillful , however, to investigate whether what the main factor